1|00/2

the cuisine of fredy girardet

the cuisine of
<u>fredy girardet</u>

BY FREDY GIRARDET

with Catherine Michel

Translated and annotated by
Michael and Judith Hill

WILLIAM MORROW and COMPANY, INC. · NEW YORK

Library of Congress Cataloging in Publication Data

Girardet, Fredy, 1936-
   The cuisine of Fredy Girardet.

   Translation of: La cuisine spontanée.
   Includes index.
   1. Cookery, French.   I. Michel, Catherine.   II. Hill,
Judith.   III. Hill, Michael, 1944-   .   IV. Title.
TX719.G5713   1984   641.5944   84-6700
ISBN 0-688-03950-2

Printed in the United States of America

2 3 4 5 6 7 8 9 10

BOOK DESIGN BY LINEY LI

CONTENTS

FREDY GIRARDET

S witzerland has in Fredy Girardet an unaccustomed superstar, for this is the country
better known for expertise in the hotel business than for high gastronomy, an ex-
porter of cooks to the kitchen brigades of international "palace" hotels.

But now, on home ground, the gastronomic world is at Girardet's feet, the Jet Set
dines at his table, the press beats on his door . . . there are flashbulbs, TV cameras,
autograph-seekers, interviews! In the midst of the noisy evidence of fame, like Voltaire's
Candide, he leaves the talking to others and tends to his garden . . . the secluded space of
his imagination as *cuisinier*.

He will say, "*La cuisine* is friendship," and he believes this. He will never learn to be
worldly. He is Swiss through and through, sturdy native of the canton of Vaud whose
only, provincial sea is the mist-laden Lake of Geneva.

Before Girardet, Crissier was the most obscure of villages. It is still unchanged, ex-
ceedingly plain, a suburb surrounded by both farm lands and factories. Everyone now
knows that it is near Lausanne, not far from Geneva via the *autoroute*. At a crossroads is
the village square, and there, at the former town hall, hangs the famous sign: FREDY
GIRARDET, CUISINIER.

The dining room occupies less space than the kitchen. Nevertheless, it is a room of
fine proportions, though almost austere in its simplicity. This sometimes surprises new-
comers who associate more glitter and glamour with the image of a great restaurant. But
chez Girardet, the dining room is made in the image of the cuisine and both reflect the
man himself. The tone is uncluttered and honest, generous and harmonious. Never af-
fected and never dull, the ambiance and the food here have character, spontaneity, and
at times, too, a sense of humor.

The title of his book in French is *La cuisine spontanée*. As you will see, the recipes
are set down explicitly, so that readers may know precisely how to proceed with them.
But, once the basics are accomplished, they have an impulsive quality, a sense of im-
provisation, particularly in the last moments of preparation. This is how Girardet works
and what he means by *cuisine spontanée*. At the restaurant, the repertory is in a state of
constant change.

Fredy can eventually be persuaded to discuss his subject. He goes about it like the complete Swiss that he is, speaking at once like poet, like peasant.

"Today's rightful cuisine is the precise harmony between the produce and its cooking. To know how to cook is rudimentary, the first necessity. But skill in cooking, to produce a fine cuisine, must be applied to products only of the most excellent quality. It is the produce itself that tempts me into playing ingredients against each other and to experiment with seasonings, with the use of vegetables, with the quick reductions of cooking juices that are so much more authentic than bravura sauces.

"I do this spontaneously because routine bores me. And I do not think that routine works in the long run. It is also necessary to think of the clientele, what people want and prefer. But I do not go too far with that; I revert to doing what I want to do, the way I want to do it. And what that is depends on the realities of the moment, on the weather, above all on the ingredients available that day that tempt me. With the same products, one can do so many things, each slightly different, yet still in the same vein. I believe that is my definition of spontaneity.

"This way of working is not always easy for my staff to follow! But we are so well attuned to each other, they manage somehow to produce whatever nuances I ask for, even when we are already filling orders from the dining room. This is one of the reasons I have eighteen cooks—and every one of them is always busy—to serve sixty-odd meals at a sitting. It may be extravagant, but I cannot work any other way."

His principles are workmanship, respect for the profession, for ingredients, for truth in flavors. And, Girardet may cook as he pleases, but respect for his clientele is a law. "Above all, my customers must be pleased, for they trust us in coming here and we do not have the right to disappoint them." Visitors to a great restaurant are always disappointed if the chef is absent. Girardet therefore accepts virtually no assignments to do anything elsewhere. This, too, is a very Swiss attitude—not as well known around the world as the anonymous bank account—but very Swiss, nevertheless.

Of nouvelle cuisine, he says, "The term has lost its meaning. It has been used and abused to apply to cooking made without knowledge of basic technique, with combinations of flavors that are against nature.

"For myself, I use the term 'spontaneous' cuisine to describe 'contemporary' cuisine, because, as much as possible, what we do here is done at the last moment. We use a minimum of sauce bases, rarely even *demi-glace; fumets*, simple stocks reduced and refrigerated until they jell naturally, are better.

"Here is an example of the same approach that any home cook can become accustomed to: Save all the juices from a roast beef; the juices will keep nearly a week in the refrigerator. In a few days, when you cook a small steak, for instance, to make a sauce, reduce a little red wine with some chopped shallot, add a spoonful of the jellied meat juices, and finish by swirling in a lump of butter. This is nouvelle cuisine if you will, but it is in fact cooking with authenticity."

Is this an easy style to emulate?

"Yes and no. Simplicity can become very difficult. In this book, we have tried to explain everything, for one way of making a dish, as clearly as possible. It is very manageable. There are no unnecessary complications. Anyone who pays attention can learn by practicing. That is the thing, practice, because, to take the same example, to finish a sauce that is barely thickened, lightly buttered, so that all the elements come together, the flavors meld with each other . . . this takes a gift of handling, and some intuition, which cannot be put down on paper in so many words.''

His collection of recipes does not discuss wines; they are another subject. But those who have visited Crissier know he has a rare and subtle taste for the marriage of food and wine. For his cooking, he prefers wines light, fresh, and young. Crissier is located in a region of vineyards that are among the finest in Switzerland. It is within a stone's throw of the terraced vineyards of Lavaux, the souce of the famous Dézaley. Girardet is a dedicated ambassador of Swiss wines. They make up more than a quarter of his *carte*, which includes classic whites made with the chasselas, the Swiss national grape, and includes also labels of greater rarity; Petite Arvine, Humagne, Riesling of the canton of Valais, and a few *cuvées* made especially for him, such as the Traminer d'Yvorne, which he likes to introduce to you as an apéritif.

Those who are interested enough in his judgment not to be apprehensive about the possible cost leave the choice of wines that will best suit the dishes they have ordered up to him. This writer has unforgettable memories of a ragout of lobster with a Trotanoy of a good year and of a Château Chalon with a *cassolette* of truffles and cardoons.

Did Fredy Girardet ever dream, in earlier years, of such extraordinary success? If he did, it is unlikely that he spoke of it. He remains very reserved, like many a Swiss, like many solid citizens of integrity and strong attachment to the soil. He is retiring in the manner of the very proud.

He does have a reply: "One can only do well what one loves."

Fredy Girardet has never worked in anyone else's great restaurant. After having observed his father at work in his local *bistrot*, Fredy went on to a thorough and uninteresting apprenticeship in Lausanne. He was still young when he returned to help in the kitchen of the family business. It was a very modest establishment, offering staple *plats du jour*, omelettes, *charcuterie*. Its peak of luxury was tournedos of beef with morels. It was housed in a portion of the same building, the *hôtel de ville* of Crissier, that is now occupied in its entirety by the prestigious Restaurant Girardet. In those days, Fredy preferred soccer (*le football*) to cooking, by a long shot. His mother frequently sent emissaries to get him off the playing field and back to the kitchen and to duty.

When Fredy was scarcely twenty, the father died and Fredy found himself head of the family, in a serious position of responsibility and burdened by a total lack of interest in the profession he had inherited. But, for many years, his mother had dealt with the clientele, only in this work would she be happy . . .

Here was a crisis of conscience. It was resolved by a brief illness followed by a trip to France and a *coup de foudre*, the thunderclap that is the French expression for falling irretrievably in love. It was a culinary event that made possible the Girardet we know today.

A tradesman, client of the Crissier *bistrot* and amateur of wines, took young Fredy to Burgundy where he was introduced to fine vintages and to a vineyard owner of perception, Jacques Parent, who in turn befriended the young cook and took him to dine *chez* Bocuse and the brothers Troisgros.

It was, totally, a revelation. So this was what cooking could be!

The time was 1968. Given what he had learned and tasted, especially with the Troisgros, he started his own long and solitary researches, months of trial and error and of emotion—for he now had faith and knew he had found what he wanted to do. Because he had the talent, the will, and need to strive for perfection, like an explosion the incipient Girardet style emerged. *Il a fait école*—another expression: He went to the head of the class. On his own.

In 1969, he borrowed to buy the town hall in which the *bistrot* had been for so long. (It was common practice in Swiss towns for such a building to be occupied by local businesses as well as by the offices of the village administration.) He made in the back a small, new dining room, keeping the *bistrot* in operation separately as well. Summer after summer, the vacation months were spent in more remodeling.

In 1974, at last his name began to be known in Paris. In 1975, the Gault Millau guide awarded him its "*Clef d'Or*." The *Guide Michelin* did nothing for him, and still has not, for there is no Michelin guide for Switzerland. It is obvious by now that recognition from Michelin is unnecessary.

Many more changes took place at Crissier. The dining room came to the front of the *hôtel de ville*, displacing the old *bistrot* entirely. The kitchens doubled their space and equipment. In 1977, at last all the offices on the upper story were vacated and the Girardet family had their building to themselves.

One must always remember the family in considering the phenomenon of Fredy Girardet. He has a love, even a cult, of family that is at the root of his philosophy of living. "If families were more united, if love of one's neighbor were founded in all of us first by the love of those who are closest to us, the world would function better, there would be less corruption, there would be fewer wars . . ."

One cannot gainsay him. Fredy lives in a familial world. There is his marvelous mother, still energetic and hard at work, smiling, attentive to all, and touchingly proud of her son. There is his wife, Muriel, whom he adores, a woman of grace and elegance, who miraculously survived a bicycle accident in 1981. Surgery and the will to live were part of the miracle, but it began with the love and support of the family. And there is his daughter Rachel, who resembles him unbelievably, and whom he watches as she grows up as only fathers can do. This is the family. It is sacrosanct and a bastion. Even friends remain outside.

All this is important, because the unquestioned loyalty of the traditional family circle gives Girardet the haven in which to marshal his strength and nurture his inspiration. His hobbies are secondary, but very much with him—he cycles thousands of kilometers in a year, skis, and runs to keep fit and to not gain weight. Weight! How he dreads it, and will not allow it. And there is also modern art, architecture, fine furniture, but especially paintings which he buys on impulse, paintings which always seem to have a likeness to him, or, rather, to his cuisine.

Fortunate in his family, fortunate in his gift for his profession, surrounded by a tremendous crew of young chefs who are passionate about their work, dedicated to his culinary principles, and intensely proud of working with him—is Fredy Girardet, citizen of Switzerland, born in Lausanne on November 17, 1936, a happy man? He is a Scorpio. To the extent that the pursuit of perfection leaves room for happiness, doubtless he is happy. May he, in any event, always remain what he is.

CATHERINE MICHEL

June 22, 1982

Girardet menu cover
designed by Julien van der Wal

PRACTICAL ADVICE

To make the recipes easy to follow, they have been written in the most concise manner possible, though they include every necessary detail. Too many sentences, too much text can do more to confuse the amateur cook than to help, making a recipe sound more complicated than it is.

Given this brevity of style, you should note certain conventions we have observed in presenting the recipes, before you begin to cook.

I. Organizing the Work

That some recipes may take quite a bit of time to execute is not in itself the point. The important thing is to know the time that needs to be allowed shortly before the dish is served. It is always brief. Professionals are very precise about this, and it is invaluable for home cooks to learn how they do it.

The kitchen staff of a restaurant begins work at eight o'clock in the morning, but the preparation of the actual dishes does not begin until the first orders come from the dining room at about twelve-thirty. By then (and before having their own lunch at eleven), the chefs have finished their *mise en place*. This is a traditional expression of chefs and may sound esoteric. It is merely practical and means to take the preparation of ingredients as far as it can go, well ahead of time—all the boning, peeling, shelling, blanching, cutting, chopping. In a restaurant, each dish can then be cooked to order and served promptly, without keeping customers waiting unduly.

At home, for guests, you surely are not concerned if an hour or several early in the day have been spent in preparation. What counts is that you are ready and know exactly what needs to be done before you sit down to dinner. To make it easier for you, we have sometimes included more steps in the advance preparations than a professional might think necessary.

The recipe format is designed so that you can identify each stage of a recipe quickly on the page. The form it takes in translation to English is set out on page 29.

II. The Ingredients, the Seasoning, the Cooking

These are the essential elements. Fredy Girardet has an innate sense of how to use them. We who are not so gifted must learn to do three things:

· To *taste, taste,* and *taste again!* This is imperative to gauge the cooking times of vegetables and to adjust the seasoning of sauces. You cannot measure seasonings by rote, nor can you cook by relying only on a kitchen timer.

· You must also *look:* The contours, the color, the sheen of fish fillets, for instance, can tell you how nearly done they are.

· And you must *touch:* When you press fish or meat with your finger, they are softest and least resilient when they are raw. This changes as they become cooked just as they should be and changes still more as they overcook. Start by getting the feel of the raw ingredient and compare that with the way it feels when you have succeeded in cooking it perfectly.

Cooking times are difficult to give in a recipe, since they depend on variables—the quality, age, and freshness of ingredients. Cooking at high heat, and therefore briefly, as Girardet does, is the most trustworthy method. If your ingredients are the best you can find, the cooking times given in the recipes should be dependable guides, assuming one important point—that your oven temperature gauge tells the truth!

III. Certain Things Are Assumed

In order not to clutter the recipes with instructions for the obvious, we have left it to your common sense to remember these rules:

· All ingredients prepared ahead for the *mise en place* must be protected from drying out and refrigerated. Vegetables that have been peeled, cut, sliced, chopped, as well as herbs, are put in containers with tightly fitting lids. Fish, meat, and poultry, filleted or trimmed and ready to cook, and seafoods, removed from their shells, should be well wrapped in plastic film.

· Ingredients must not be taken directly from the refrigerator for cooking. Cooking times are given for ingredients at room temperature.

· Unless a recipe directs otherwise, ingredients are seasoned just before they are cooked. This applies as well to red meats, despite all the foolishness to the contrary in so many cookbooks. It is simply not correct to season meat only at the end of cooking. Raw salt, in particular, is aggressive, while salt that has entered into the cooking brings out the natural flavor of foods. What you must do is to season lightly at the beginning, and taste and adjust the seasoning at the end of cooking.

- Use only the best unsalted butter.
- Use only peppercorns freshly ground in a pepper mill.
- Use only good wine vinegars, and for oil use peanut oil unless some other kind is specified.
- Preheat the oven far enough in advance so that it will reach the specified temperature by the time you intend to use it.
- Skillets, saucepans, and the like must be of a size to hold pieces of meat, fish, or poultry in one layer, with just enough but not too much room to spare.
- Meat and poultry are always improved by resting for a few minutes in a warm place before they are served.
- Becoming nervous and agitated in the kitchen never helps anything. Take your time. Guests who love good food will be more than happy to wait for a good dish and between courses.
- Finally, the advice that is always given, and always applies: Before you begin to cook, read and reread the recipe until you know it almost by heart.

IV. *La cuisine spontanée*

What Fredy Girardet means by this has already been explained, but one has to see him in action in his kitchen to grasp the full meaning. He works with incredible ease with his ingredients, with flavors, sauces, and garnishes. It is perfectly apt to say that he works as a painter does with colors from a palette, according to the inspiration of the moment. And he can foretell the tastes and textures he is creating even as he goes about the process of invention.

These are gifts the rest of us do not have and to which this book cannot do justice. Had we tried to record five or six variations for each recipe, he would have invented more of them by the following morning! We have had to be content with one version of each recipe, set down as clearly as possible.

But the lesson is obvious, that a recipe is a point of departure and it can be a good thing, once you have made it successfully, to reconsider the recipe and see what it may suggest to your own imagination. It will be a revelation to copy exactly what this chef of genius offers you in his book, but how fascinating it would be to play his game, to experiment, even at the price of some imperfect results. To those who set out to understand Fredy Girardet's talent and techniques seriously, a way to go on to their own inventions will present itself; that is the hope implicit in the book.

We wish you many successes, and *bon appétit*!

C.M.

NOTES ON THE TRANSLATION

T he procedures and organization of the recipes in the original French by Fredy Girardet and Catherine Michel are followed faithfully in this translation. As we cooked each dish, we found that the method of attack was always carefully thought out to be the most sensible possible. Most chefs work according to a similar pattern, doing all the preparation well ahead, so that the final cooking is quick enough to finish a dish shortly after it has been ordered. However, this practical professional's approach has rarely, if ever before, been so clear in a chef's written recipes. The headings of each section of a recipe organize the work as follows:

PREPARATIONS:

This is the *mise en place* and includes everything you can do ahead, often as much as half a day and always at least one hour in advance.

FINISHING:

This heading indicates that the remainder of the method (*finitions*), the final cooking, will take no more than 10 minutes.

COOKING:

This is the heading used when the remainder of the method will take more than 10 minutes (*cuisson et finitions* in the French). The longer cooking times vary. In Fredy Girardet's rapid style of cooking, they are seldom more than 30 minutes.

PRESENTATION:

Most of Girardet's recipes are designed for plate service, a hallmark of *nouvelle cuisine.*

COMMENTS following the recipes and printed in the usual text type are the comments of Fredy Girardet. The **NOTES** printed in *italics* are ours.

In the lists of ingredients, a preparation that you must have on hand before you begin to assemble the recipe is printed in **boldface** type, with a page reference to the chapter of basic recipes at the end of the book. There are surprisingly few such references. Also entered, in parentheses, are references to the **NOTES** and **COMMENTS** that you should read before you plan to make a recipe.

Ingredients and Shopping by Mail

When this translation was first begun, it was a question whether recipes for which ingredients are hard to find in this country should be included. It seemed too bad to delete anything, since the object of the book is to present a true portrait of how Fredy Girardet works. Before we finished, more and more ingredients became available. American fresh wild mushrooms are now being marketed, there was a virtual price war on fresh truffles in New York City, and, amazingly, duck foie gras is being produced in the United States. Such ingredients are costly and still not easy to get. Recipes requiring them may have to be passed over, but we were able to get the ingredients for almost every one. In the end, not a single recipe was deleted. We made them all.

With caution, we have suggested substitutions when they seemed valid. Of course, the results are different from the Girardet originals.

FOIE GRAS:

American fresh raw duck livers are of excellent quality. They were not yet available to retail customers when we made the recipes, and so we used a wholesale source and successfully tested them all with American foie gras. Since then a few suppliers have begun to fill retail orders. Surely it will not be long before the better markets begin to carry fresh foie gras.

Top-quality domestic duck foie-gras terrine cooked to the "mi-cuit" stage is now available and is infinitely preferable to imported canned foie gras, which must be heated to such a high temperature in the canning process that the distinctive texture of the fresh liver is spoiled. An excellent mail-order source is Gerard's Haute Cuisine, Mountain Road, Stowe, Vermont 95672.

TRUFFLES AND TRUFFLE JUICE:

Fresh truffles are available during the season (about mid-December to mid-March) in the better specialty shops of large cities. You can be sure the shops let their customers know when they arrive! Frozen truffles, which are much more aromatic and flavorful than the canned, can be used in place of fresh. They have just recently become available and should soon reach the specialty shops. For information on where to buy them, contact Agri-truffle, Star Route 1A, Box 45A, Dripping Springs, Texas 78620. During the season you can get fresh truffles by mail order from the same source.

Do not peel fresh or frozen truffles. They only need to be thoroughly rinsed and gently brushed, with a very soft "mushroom brush," if you have one; scrubbing truffles with a stiff vegetable brush would be disastrous.

Truffle juice is difficult to find in retail markets. Two mail-order sources are De Choix Specialty Foods Company, 58-25 52nd Avenue, Woodside, New York 11377 and Flying Foods International, Inc., 158-08 Rockaway Boulevard, Jamaica, New York 11454.

CRAYFISH:

Crayfish are caught commercially in Louisiana and from Washington state to California. They are flown, live, to urban markets all over the country and can be ordered by mail. One mail-order source is: California Sunshine Fine Foods, Inc., 144 King Street, San Francisco, California 94107. See page 39 for preparing live crayfish.

Fresh shelled crayfish tails on ice that have been blanched in boiling water for a few seconds are also marketed, especially in Louisiana. If you have access to them, study the recipes that call for crayfish; in many (though not all), you can find a point at which you can proceed with blanched tails instead of starting out with live crayfish.

LOBSTERETTES:

These we were not able to get. Lobsterettes, or *langoustines*, sometimes called saltwater crayfish or Dublin Bay prawns, can be found off the coast of the United States from New Jersey to Florida and in the Caribbean, but they are seldom marketed. They are a small relative of the lobster. Shrimp, a commonly suggested substitute because of the confusion created by the name Dublin Bay prawn, have a very different texture and flavor. The substitution that stays closest to the flavor of the original is lobster, and the weight of lobster tail to substitute is suggested wherever lobsterettes appear in a recipe.

SPRING ONIONS:

This is the term we have used when Girardet called for small, round bulb onions with their fresh green tops resembling the tops of scallions. We also found them in American markets by the name of "new onions," as the French say it—*oignon nouveau* (and *en tige*—with the green tops). By whatever name, such onions are seasonal; we shopped for onions of the mildest flavor when there was no hope of finding spring onions.

We would like to thank Patricia Hesler, who typed perfect pages from hieroglyphics, and Barbara Sause, who helped test the pastry recipes. This was a truly wonderful project, and we are grateful to Morrow editor Narcisse Chamberlain for giving it to us to do. In the course of cooking these recipes, we became convinced that Fredy Girardet is a genius.

MICHAEL AND JUDITH HILL
January 15, 1984

to my mother
and to my father

potages

SOUPS

Crème d'asperges vertes
aux morilles

ASPARAGUS SOUP WITH MORELS

TO SERVE 4:

6 medium asparagus spears
8 thin asparagus spears
3 ounces (about ¾ cup) morels (see **NOTE**)
1 shallot
6 tablespoons butter
1 cup heavy cream
Salt, pepper, and cayenne

PREPARATIONS:

Snap the tough ends off all the asparagus and then cut the 8 thin spears just below the tips. Cook the whole medium-size asparagus spears and the stalks from the thin spears in boiling salted water for 10 minutes. Remove and set aside. Add the 8 tips to the boiling water and cook until just tender, about 5 minutes. Remove the tips and set aside, and reserve the cooking liquid. Wash the morels well and cut them in quarters. Chop the shallot.

Heat 3 tablespoons of the butter in a pan, add two thirds of the chopped shallot, and let it brown. Add the 6 medium asparagus spears and 1 cup of their cooking liquid to the pan and bring to a boil. Add the cream and cook at a rapid boil for 2 minutes. Remove from the heat, let cool a moment, and then put the liquid, along with 2 tablespoons of the butter, into a food processor and purée it. Strain the purée through a fine sieve back into the pan and season it with salt, pepper, and cayenne.

FINISHING:

Put the morels, the rest of the chopped shallot, and the remaining 1 tablespoon of butter in a small saucepan. Salt them and cook over low heat until all their juices are rendered. At that moment they're done; remove them from the heat. While the morels are cooking, reheat the asparagus soup. Bring the remaining asparagus cooking liquid to a boil and plunge the 8 tips into the liquid briefly to reheat.

Serve the soup in shallow bowls. Put a quarter of the morels in the middle of each bowl and add two asparagus tips as garnish.

NOTE: *If fresh morels are not available, use ½ ounce (about ½ cup) dried morels, first soaked in warm water for at least half an hour. Ed.*

Court-bouillon
d'écrevisses à l'aneth et au beluga

CRAYFISH BOUILLON WITH DILL AND CAVIAR

TO SERVE 4:

24 to 40 large (about 2½ to 4 pounds) live crayfish (see page
   31 and **COMMENTS**)
¼ tomato
1 leaf green cabbage
1 branch fresh dill
½ lime
Small knob gingerroot
1 cup **vegetable bouillon** (page 228)
3 ounces (⅜ cup) champagne
Salt and pepper
2 tablespoons butter
2 ounces Beluga caviar

PREPARATIONS:

Let the crayfish cleanse themselves for at least 1 hour in a large bowl of cold water, securely covered so that you won't find them running all over the kitchen. Peel and seed the tomato and cut it into enough fine dice to make 1 tablespoon. Blanch the cabbage leaf in salted boiling water for 5 minutes, remove it, refresh with cold water, and then drain. Remove the large central vein and cut the leaf into enough ½-inch-square pieces to make 1 tablespoon.

Chop enough dill to make 1 teaspoon. Grate one third of the zest from the lime half and squeeze the juice. Peel the ginger and grate enough of it to make ½ teaspoon.

Bring a large pot of water to a boil. Drain the crayfish and plunge them into the boiling water. After 2 minutes, remove the crayfish, drain, and let cool a bit so that they won't burn your fingers. Remove the tail meat and, if you like, gently pull out the vein. Keep the tails at room temperature.

FINISHING:

Put the vegetable bouillon into a pan. Add the champagne, dill, tomato, and cabbage. Flavor the bouillon with the lime juice and zest, the grated ginger, and salt and pepper. Bring it to a boil and then remove it from the heat.

Put the crayfish tails into the bouillon for a minute to reheat them. Remove them with a skimmer or slotted spoon, stir the butter into the consommé, taste for seasoning and correct if necessary.

PRESENTATION:

Serve lukewarm in shallow bowls. Arrange the crayfish tails in a star pattern and pour the consommé over them. Put a tablespoon of caviar in the center of each bowl.

COMMENTS: The number of crayfish used depends on how heavy the rest of the menu is.

Use the crayfish bodies and shells to make crayfish butter (page 231).

NOTES: *The crayfish must be live. Discard any dead ones.*

Boil the crayfish in two batches if necessary. Be sure the water returns to a boil before adding the second batch. Ed.

CRAYFISH MINESTRONE

TO SERVE 4:

32 (about 3 pounds) live crayfish (see page 31)
4 small carrots
4 small turnips
2 shallots
2 garlic cloves
20 leaves lovage (see **NOTES**)
Salt and pepper
2 pinches cayenne
10 tablespoons butter
8 large pods fava (or broad) beans (see **NOTES**)
2 teaspoons olive oil
¾ cup **crayfish stock** (page 230)
4 teaspoons **crayfish butter** (page 231)
2½ cups **vegetable bouillon** (page 228)

PREPARATIONS:

Let the crayfish cleanse themselves for at least 1 hour in a large bowl of cold water, securely covered. Peel the carrots and turnips and cut them into very thin slices. Mince the shallots and the garlic cloves. Also chop the lovage.

NOTES: *The crayfish must be live. Discard any dead ones.*

Boil the crayfish in two batches if necessary. Be sure the water returns to a boil before adding the second batch. Ed.

Throw the crayfish into a large pot of boiling water. Remove them after 1 minute. Let them cool a bit and then remove the tail meat and, if you like, gently pull out the veins. Arrange the crayfish tails in a shallow baking dish, season them with salt and a pinch of cayenne, and dot with 2 tablespoons of the butter.

Remove the fava beans from their pods, cook them 2 minutes in salted boiling water, and then drain them and remove their skins.

In a saucepan over medium heat, brown half the chopped garlic and chopped shallot in a teaspoon of the olive oil. Add the crayfish stock and crayfish butter, bring to a boil, and let the mixture reduce for 3 to 4 minutes. Add 4 tablespoons of the butter and continue to cook, whisking, for 30 seconds. Remove the pan from the heat, add salt and a pinch of cayenne to the stock, and then set it aside until ready to incorporate it into the soup.

FINISHING:

Heat the oven to 400°F. In a saucepan over medium heat, brown the rest of the shallots and garlic in the remaining teaspoon of olive oil. Add the carrots and turnips and cook for 30 seconds, stirring. Add the vegetable bouillon, bring to a boil, and boil gently for 5 minutes. Add the remaining 4 tablespoons of butter and whisk for 1 minute while the soup continues to boil. Finally add the beans, the reduced crayfish stock and butter mixture, and the chopped lovage. Taste for seasoning. Keep the soup warm while you cook the crayfish for 2 minutes in the preheated oven.

PRESENTATION:

Ladle the soup into shallow bowls and mound eight crayfish in the center of each bowl.

NOTES: *Lovage is a traditional English and American herb that has fallen out of use. It is still much used in Switzerland, especially to flavor soups. It is a member of the celery family and has the flavor of lemon-touched, slightly bitter celery. If it's unavailable, substitute celery leaves and a pinch of grated lemon zest in this soup.*

Fava beans can be found in Italian, Middle Eastern, and other specialty markets. Lima beans can be substituted in this recipe. You may need to cook them longer, up to 20 minutes depending on their age. Then remove skins and use as directed. Ed.

Crème de champignons
des bois aux pluches de cerfeuil

WILD MUSHROOM SOUP WITH CHERVIL LEAVES

TO SERVE 4:

¹⁄₂ pound cèpes or other wild mushroom (see **COMMENT** and **NOTE**)
1 small shallot
1 small garlic clove
3 sprigs chervil
1 tablespoon peanut oil
1 ¹⁄₂ tablespoons butter
Salt, and cayenne
1 ¹⁄₄ cups heavy cream
¹⁄₄ lemon

PREPARATIONS:

Clean and trim the mushrooms and mince them. Mince the shallot and the garlic clove. Pluck the chervil leaves from the stems. You should have 1 to 2 teaspoons leaves.

Put the oil in a frying pan over high heat. Add the minced mushrooms and, when they have rendered their juices, add the butter and the minced garlic and shallot. Salt and pepper, mix together, and continue cooking until the mushrooms are nicely browned. Remove half of the mushroom mixture from the pan and reserve as garnish.

Add the cream to the remaining half of the mushroom mixture, scrape the bottom of the pan to detach any cooked-on juices, and then pour the mixture into a saucepan. Bring it to a boil and let it boil for 2 minutes. Remove it from the heat and purée in a food processor.

FINISHING:

Put the mushroom purée into a saucepan, thin it with water until the consistency of thick soup, and season it with salt, cayenne, and lemon juice to taste. Now bring it to a boil and keep warm. Reheat the mushroom mixture set aside earlier.

PRESENTATION:

Ladle the soup into small bowls. Put a quarter of the mushroom garnish in the center of each serving and then sprinkle the chervil over the soup.

NOTE: *One and a half ounces (about 1 ½ cups) dried cèpes, first soaked in warm water for at least half an hour, can be used in place of the fresh mushrooms. Ed.*

Soupe tiède de moules
aux carottes nouvelles et á l'aneth

MUSSEL SOUP WITH CARROTS AND DILL

TO SERVE 4:

1 pound small carrots
1 small shallot
3 cups small mussels
1 branch dill
5 tablespoons butter
¾ cup white wine
Salt and pepper

PREPARATIONS:

Slice the carrots. Mince the shallot. Scrub the mussels and remove the beards. Pull enough dill from the dill branch to make ½ teaspoon dill leaves.

Put the carrots in a small saucepan with a pinch of salt and enough water to barely cover them. Boil them until they are tender but still firm; the time needed will vary according to the freshness of the vegetables but should be a maximum of 10 minutes. When the carrots are done, remove from the heat and reserve both carrots and cooking liquid for later use.

To open the mussels, melt 3 tablespoons of the butter in a good-size pan over medium-low heat, add the minced shallot and let it cook 1 minute without browning. Raise the heat to medium, add the mussels and wine, and cover. Shake the pan every minute or so and watch the mussels carefully so that you remove the pan from the heat as soon as they open, which should take only a few minutes; otherwise they will overcook and become tough. When the mussels have opened, pour the cooking liquid through a cheesecloth-lined strainer into a saucepan. Shell the mussels over the strainer to catch every bit of their juices.

Cut a scant ½ cup of the carrot slices into thin julienne strips. Add the rest of the carrots and ¼ cup of their cooking liquid to the mussel cooking liquid. Bring this to a boil and then cook it gently for 5 minutes. Add the remaining 2 tablespoons of butter, let the butter melt, and then remove the pan from the heat. Put the contents of the pan in a food processor or food mill and purée. Strain the purée into a saucepan through a sieve so that you have a perfectly smooth cream. If it is too thick, add the remaining carrot cooking liquid and water, if necessary, to make a thick soup.

FINISHING:

Put the mussels and any juices that have accumulated into the pan with the cream soup; reheat them slowly and remove the pan from the heat as soon as the soup starts to boil.

PRESENTATION:

Use four warm shallow bowls. In each one, put a quarter of the mussels, cover them with the carrot soup, and then garnish with the tiny carrot julienne and the dill.

Crème de persil frisé
à la fricassée de grenouilles

PARSLEY SOUP WITH FROG LEG FRICASSEE

TO SERVE 4:

24 frog legs, about 1 pound in all
2 bunches parsley
2 small shallots
5 tablespoons butter
⅓ cup white wine
⅔ cup **vegetable bouillon** (page 228) or water
1¼ cups heavy cream
Salt and pepper
¼ teaspoon flour
A few drops peanut oil

PREPARATIONS:

Bone the frog legs by slitting them along both sides and pulling out the bones, making sure that you get all the meat from them. Reserve both bones and meat. Pluck enough parsley leaves from the stems to make 4 cups, unpacked (2 ounces). Mince the shallots.

Melt 2 tablespoons of the butter in a saucepan and add to it the frog leg bones and half the minced shallots. Cook them over low heat for 3 to 5 minutes, stirring and occasionally pressing on the bones. Be careful not to let either the shallots or the bones brown.

Now moisten the mixture with the wine and the vegetable bouillon or water. Bring this to a boil and continue boiling for 5 to 8 minutes. Press down on the bones from time to time so that they render all their juices. While the bones are cooking, prepare the parsley by cooking it in boiling water until it is tender, about 5 minutes. Then drain it, put in a saucepan, and set aside.

Strain the frog leg stock, pushing firmly on the bones to get all the juice. Now pour the stock into the pan with the parsley and all but 1 teaspoon of the 1¼ cups cream. Bring to a boil, remove it from the heat, and purée in a food processor. Strain the resulting soup back into the pan and set it aside.

FINISHING:

Put the pieces of frog leg meat in a bowl, salt and pepper them, moisten them with the reserved teaspoon of cream, and then sprinkle the flour over them. Mix them well until they're covered with a sticky cream. Heat a non-stick frying pan with a few drops of oil over high heat, put the frog leg meat in it, and keep them moving briskly with a wooden spatula so that they remain separated. After about 1 minute when they begin to brown, add the rest of the minced shallots and 2 tablespoons of the butter and continue cooking them over high heat another minute until they're nicely browned all over.

Salt and pepper the parsley soup, add the remaining 1 tablespoon of butter, and bring to a boil.

PRESENTATION:

Pour the soup into bowls and mound a quarter of the frog legs in the middle of each bowl.

Parmentière de moules aux poireaux

POTATO SOUP WITH MUSSELS AND LEEKS

TO SERVE 4:

1 small leek
½ pound potatoes
1 small shallot
1 quart small mussels
3 tablespoons butter
¾ cup white wine
¼ cup cold water
Salt and pepper
1 pinch cayenne

PREPARATIONS:

Wash the leek, cut off the dark green end, and mince enough of the white and light-green parts to make ½ cup. Cook the potatoes in salted water until tender, peel, and put them through a food mill or sieve to purée them. You should have ¾ cup. Chop the shallot. Wash the mussels and remove their beards.

In a large pan, melt the butter over medium-low heat. Add the shallot, soften for a minute without browning, and then add the white wine and the mussels. Cover the pan, raise the heat to medium, and cook, shaking the pan from time to time, until the mussels open. It should take only a few minutes. Be careful to cook the mussels no longer than necessary to open them; otherwise they will overcook and become tough. Pour the mussels and their cooking liquid into another pan through a cheesecloth-lined strainer. Now remove the mussels from their shells, set the shelled mussels aside, and reserve their cooking liquid.

FINISHING:

Add the cold water to the pan with the mussel cooking liquid, put the minced leek into the pan, and cook it over medium heat for 3 or 4 minutes. Now add the ¾ cup potato purée to the soup a bit at a time, whisking to mix well. If it is too thick after the potatoes have been mixed in, add water to make a thick soup. Now add the mussels, bring the soup just to a boil, remove it from the heat, and season with salt, pepper, and a pinch of cayenne.

PRESENTATION:

Divide the mussels equally among warm shallow bowls and pour a portion of the soup into each bowl.

Crème de tomates au basilic

TOMATO SOUP WITH BASIL

TO SERVE 4:

1¼ pounds (4 medium) ripe red tomatoes
Six ¼-inch slices from a 2½- to 3-inch-diameter loaf of day-old
    bread, or 3 slices from a larger loaf
2 garlic cloves
1 spring onion (see page 31)
8 leaves fresh basil
½ bay leaf
2 cloves
1¼ cups heavy cream
Salt and pepper
1½ tablespoons butter

PREPARATIONS:

Peel the tomatoes. Seed half of them and cut into small dice for the garnish. Put the other half into the food processor. Purée them and then strain the purée and set aside. You should have about 1 cup of the strained tomatoes.

Heat the oven to 300°F. Cut 1 of the garlic cloves in half and rub the bread slices with the garlic. Cut the slices into ¼-inch cubes and put the cubes in the preheated oven for 5 to 10 minutes until dry and crisp. Cut the root and most of the top off the onion and peel the remaining garlic clove. Cut the basil leaves into fine shreds.

Pour the cup of tomato juice into a saucepan, add the ½ bay leaf, cloves, the whole peeled garlic cloves, and the onion. Bring to a boil and then let cook over medium heat, uncovered, for about 10 minutes until the tomato liquid has been reduced by half. Remove and discard the bay leaf, garlic, onion, and cloves.

FINISHING:

Add the cream to the tomato liquid and bring this to a boil, whisking. Salt and pepper the soup, remove the pan from the heat, and whisk the butter into the soup. Whir the soup in a food processor to emulsify it and then pour it back into the pan. Add the tomato dice and the shredded basil leaves and bring the soup to a boil once more.

PRESENTATION:

Serve in shallow bowls with the garlic croûtons as an accompaniment to be sprinkled over the soup.

Soupe de légumes
aux petits coquillages

VEGETABLE SOUP WITH SHELLFISH

TO SERVE 4:

Tender green part of 1 leek
1 small turnip
1 medium carrot
1 leaf savoy cabbage
1 tomato
1 spring onion (see page 31)
½ garlic clove
2 cups small mussels
2 cups small clams
4 sea scallops
3 tablespoons olive oil
½ cup **vegetable bouillon** (page 228)
¼ cup white wine
2½ tablespoons butter

PREPARATIONS:

Wash the vegetables and peel them if necessary. Cut up the leek, turnip, carrot, and cabbage peasant style, in other words in squares or triangles about ½ inch a side and ⅛ inch thick. Peel and seed the tomato and cut it into very small dice. Mince the onion and the garlic.

Wash the mussels and clams and remove the beards from the mussels. Cut the scallops into 3 or 4 slices and then cut each slice into small sticks.

Heat 1 tablespoon of the olive oil in a frying pan and then put in the clams and ¼ cup of the vegetable bouillon. Simmer the clams only until they open and remove them from the heat immediately or they will become tough. Set them aside and strain the cooking liquid through a cheesecloth-lined sieve into a small saucepan. You'll use the lined sieve again later.

Put the white wine and the remaining ¼ cup vegetable bouillon in a saucepan over low heat and add the mussels. Check the mussels carefully so that you remove them as soon as they open; otherwise they, like the clams, will toughen. When they're done, remove them and pour the liquid through the sieve lined with cheesecloth into the pan of clam broth. Reduce the liquids by boiling down to half their volume and reserve. Shell the mussels and clams, keeping them separate, and set aside until you're ready to finish the soup.

FINISHING:

Heat the remaining 2 tablespoons of olive oil in a saucepan over medium heat and add the minced onion and garlic. Let them cook a minute, and then pour in the reserved shellfish cooking liquid and bring to a boil over high heat. Now put in the pieces of leek, turnip, cabbage, and carrot and cook them very rapidly for 2 minutes. Remove the pan from the heat and stir in the butter. Add the tomato dice and the mussels, bring the soup to a boil, and immediately remove it from the heat. Add the scallop sticks and the clams and check the seasoning.

PRESENTATION:

Divide the soup and the shellfish among warm shallow bowls.

terrines

TERRINES

———— ❖ ————

Gelée de poulette

CHICKEN ASPIC WITH FOIE GRAS

TO SERVE 8:

One 2- to 2½-pound chicken
Salt and pepper
2 sprigs tarragon
2½ tablespoons white-wine vinegar
2 fennel bulbs
1½ cups **chicken aspic** (page 235)
⅓ pound **Terrine of Duck Foie Gras** (page 54 and page 55)
4 teaspoons peanut oil

PREPARATIONS:

Heat the oven to 425°F. Season the chicken with salt and pepper and set it on its side in a roasting pan. Roast it in the preheated oven for 30 minutes, 12 minutes on each side and the remaining 6 minutes on its back. The meat should still be pink. Set aside until cool enough to handle. Carve the chicken into pieces and then remove all the skin and bones. Try not to spoil the shape of the pieces too much. Put all the chicken into a bowl and season with salt and pepper. Chop the tarragon leaves and sprinkle a good pinch of them over the chicken. Moisten the chicken with 2 tablespoons of the vinegar and let it macerate at least 1 hour at room temperature.

Cut the fennel bulbs in half and cook 3 of the halves in salted boiling water until they're tender, about 20 minutes. Drain them, let them cool, and then cut them into slices ½ inch thick. Reserve the remaining half fennel bulb to use raw as garnish.

Put the chicken aspic in a pan and warm it over low heat until it melts. Remove it from the heat and add the remaining tarragon. Season with salt and pepper. Remove the coating of fat from the foie gras and cut the foie gras into ¼-inch slices.

Pour enough of the melted aspic into a 1½-quart terrine to make a ¼-inch layer and then refrigerate it until set, 30 minutes to an hour. Slice the chicken pieces, if necessary, so that they aren't more than ½ inch thick. When the aspic has set, arrange a layer of the chicken pieces on top of it. On top of the chicken layer, put half the foie gras slices. Now put a layer of the fennel slices on top of the foie gras and then layer the rest of the foie gras slices over the fennel. Put the remaining chicken pieces on as the last layer and fill the terrine with the remaining aspic. Refrigerate overnight.

Cut the half raw fennel bulb into thin slices. Whisk together the remaining ½ tablespoon vinegar, the oil, and salt and pepper. Toss the fennel with this vinaigrette.

PRESENTATION:

Run a knife around edge of terrine to loosen it. Cut into thick slices with a very sharp thin knife and remove each slice carefully with a metal spatula. Put the slices on individual plates and decorate each plate with a few slices of the dressed fennel.

Terrine de poissons
du Léman à la ciboulette

LAKE FISH TERRINE WITH CHIVES

TO SERVE 8 TO 10:

½ pound trout fillets (see **NOTE**)
1 egg white
1 cup heavy cream
Salt and pepper
1 pinch cayenne
4 limes
6 ounces salmon trout fillets
6 ounces perch fillets
¼ pound chives

PREPARATIONS:

Purée the trout fillets and egg white in the food processor. Chill the mixture at least 30 minutes in the refrigerator. Put a good layer of ice cubes in a large bowl and put a smaller metal bowl containing the fish purée on top of the ice. With a wooden spoon, stir in the cream, 1 to 2 tablespoons at a time. Season the mixture with about ½ teaspoon salt, ¼ teaspoon pepper, a pinch of cayenne, and the juice of 1 lime. Refrigerate for at least 1 hour.

Cut enough thin slices from 1 of the limes to line the bottom of a 1½-quart terrine, 12 inches long. Cut the salmon trout fillets into ½-inch-wide strips. Put the salmon trout strips and the whole fillets of perch into a bowl and squeeze the juice of the 2 remaining limes over them. Mix and leave to macerate for 30 minutes. Chop the chives.

Spread a ⅛-inch layer of the trout mixture on the limes lining the terrine. Next make a layer of half the perch fillets, rolled lengthwise, and half the salmon trout strips, alternating colors. Cover the fish with half the chopped chives and then repeat with half the remaining trout mixture, the rest of the fish, the remaining chives, and finally fill the terrine with the remaining trout mixture.

Heat the oven to 350°F. Put the terrine in a baking dish or roasting pan and add hot water to come halfway up the terrine. Put the terrine, in its water bath, into the preheated oven and cook for 45 minutes. Refrigerate until chilled, at least 2 hours.

PRESENTATION:

Run a knife around the edge of the terrine, pour off excess liquid given off by the lime slices and fillets, and unmold. Serve cut crosswise into thick slices, with a homemade mayonnaise lightened with some whipped cream and flavored with chopped chives.

NOTE: *Chef Girardet makes this terrine with the local fish called féra. See* **NOTE** *page 106. Ed.*

Terrine de foie gras de canard

TERRINE OF DUCK FOIE GRAS

TO SERVE 6 TO 8:

1 pound raw duck foie gras (see page 30)
1½ teaspoons salt
¼ teaspoon white pepper
1 pinch sugar
1 teaspoon madeira

PREPARATIONS:

Let the duck liver rest for 2 hours in water that is not too cold. Then separate the lobes of the liver and carefully remove the nerves you find inside. Start at the top of the interior side of each lobe and pull gently, following the network of nerves. This may tear the liver somewhat, but it will come back together in cooking.

Put the foie gras in a shallow bowl and season with 1 ½ teaspoons salt and ¼ teaspoon white pepper. Sprinkle a pinch of sugar over the liver and then the madeira. Turn the foie gras over in the bowl several times so that it is all well seasoned. Then put it in an oval terrine, cover closely with plastic wrap, and refrigerate for 12 hours. Bring to room temperature again before cooking.

COOKING:

Set the oven at 300°F. and let heat for 30 minutes. Line the bottom of a small roasting pan with a section of newspaper folded in quarter and then put the terrine, uncovered, on top of the paper. Fill the roasting pan with cold water to come two thirds up the terrine. Put the roasting pan with the terrine in the preheated oven, turn off the oven, and leave for 35 minutes. The foie gras should be lightly cooked, warm in the center but still rosy. If your oven doesn't hold heat well and at the end of 35 minutes there is no sign of rendered fat on top of the terrine or the center is still cool, remove the terrine from the oven and reheat it to 300°F. Put the terrine in the water bath back in the oven, turn it off again, and cook for another 10 to 15 minutes.

Remove the roasting pan from the oven and hold it under a stream of cold water to cool the water bath rapidly. Now take a small board, or other firm material such as Styrofoam, cut roughly in the shape of the terrine and set it on top of the cooked liver for a few minutes, with a weight on it to press the foie gras together firmly. Remove the board before the fat congeals so that the fat can spread across the foie gras. Chill the terrine, covered, for at least 24 hours.

PRESENTATION:

Present the foie gras in the terrine and then slice ½-inch-thick pieces with a knife that has been heated in hot water. Accompany the foie gras with toasted brioche.

Terrine de
primeurs au foie gras

TERRINE OF VEGETABLES
AND FOIE GRAS

TO SERVE 8:

¾ pound carrots
¾ pound small turnips
1½ pounds broccoli
1 pound (about 5 bunches) parsley
1 pound raw duck foie gras (see page 30)
Salt and pepper
1 pinch sugar
Butter for brushing the terrine
3 ounces cooked chicken meat (from 2 small chicken breasts)
1 cup heavy cream
2 tablespoons white-wine vinegar
6 tablespoons walnut oil
Seasonal greens, for garnish

PREPARATIONS:

Peel the carrots and turnips and cut them into ¼-inch dice. Remove all the thick stems from the broccoli so that you have only the flowerets. Cut or twist the large stems off the parsley and discard or save for bouquet garni. You should have about ½ pound leaves.

Let the raw foie gras soak for at least 30 minutes in lukewarm water and then remove the nerves as described in the preceding recipe. Season the liver with salt, pepper, and a small pinch of sugar.

With a pastry brush, butter the interior of a long, narrow 1½-quart terrine. Line it completely with a sheet of aluminum foil with the shiny side down. Butter the aluminum foil and then put the prepared terrine into the refrigerator to await the assembling of the ingredients.

Bring a large pot of salted water to a boil. Cook the parsley in the boiling water for 5 minutes. Remove with a skimmer or slotted spoon, rinse in cold water, and set aside to steep in cold water for 10 minutes. Squeeze and pat dry in paper towels. Cook the carrots 5 minutes in the boiling water, remove, and refresh under cold running water. Cook the turnips for 2 minutes in the boiling water and remove and refresh them in the same way.

Finally cook the broccoli for 4 minutes and also refresh it under cold water. Set the broccoli, carrots, and turnips out on a cloth to dry.

Purée the carefully dried parsley and the cooked chicken together in the food processor. Push the mixture through a fine strainer afterward so that it is free of lumps. It is indispensable to obtain a smooth purée. Season the purée with a large pinch of salt and 20 turns of a pepper mill. Put the bowl with this purée in a larger shallow bowl of ice water and, with a wooden spatula or spoon, gradually stir in the cream, 1 to 2 tablespoons at a time. Season with salt and pepper.

Take the buttered terrine from the refrigerator and spread a thin layer of the chicken-parsley purée on the bottom, using about ¼ cup. Season all the vegetables and stir them into the remaining purée. Put half this mixture in the terrine and pack it down. Cut the foie gras into thick slices and arrange them on top of the half-filled terrine, leaving a narrow space around the edge. Fill the terrine with the rest of the vegetable, parsley, and chicken mixture. Pack it in around the sides of the layer of foie gras and mold it so it extends evenly about ½ inch above the rim of the terrine; it will shrink slightly as it cooks.

Heat the oven to 325°F. Cover the terrine with a sheet of buttered paper and set it in a heavy roasting pan. Add cold water to the pan to come two thirds up the terrine. Carefully put the terrine, in its water bath, in the preheated oven and cook until firm to the touch, about 45 minutes to 1 hour. Remove the terrine from the water bath, cool, and refrigerate, covered, at least overnight.

Make a vinaigrette by whisking together the vinegar, salt and pepper, and oil.

PRESENTATION:

Dip the bottom of the terrine in hot water for a few moments and unmold. Cut in thin slices and serve one or two slices, napped with the vinaigrette, per person. Garnish each plate with a few leaves of a seasonal green.

salades

SALADS

Salade tiède de pointes
d'asperges sauvages à la vinaigrette de truffes

WARM ASPARAGUS SALAD WITH TRUFFLE VINAIGRETTE

TO SERVE 4:

2 eggs
2 ounces fresh truffles (see **NOTE**)
60 wild asparagus or thin cultivated asparagus spears
2 tablespoons white-wine vinegar
1 teaspoon red-wine vinegar
1 tablespoon peanut oil
1 tablespoon walnut oil
2 tablespoons truffle juice (see **NOTE**)
Salt and pepper

PREPARATIONS:

Hard boil the eggs and chop them. Chop the truffles into good-size pieces. Cut the asparagus stalks off so that you have 2-inch tips and, if you're using cultivated asparagus, peel the bit of stalk left on the tip. If you have wild asparagus, you don't need to peel the spears. Save the stalks for soup or some other use. Cook the asparagus tips in salted boiling water until tender, about 5 minutes, and drain. In a small saucepan, whisk together the vinegars, oils, truffle juice, and salt and pepper to taste. Stir in the chopped eggs and truffles.

FINISHING:

Heat the vinaigrette gently over low heat. If the asparagus tips have cooled, plunge them into boiling water, remove them quickly, and drain. The salad should be served lukewarm.

PRESENTATION:

Arrange the asparagus tips on warm plates and then pour the vinaigrette over them, making sure to apportion the truffle pieces equally.

NOTE: *This is a good recipe for asparagus even without the truffles and truffle juice. See page 31 for information on truffles. Ed.*

Asperges au foie chaud en vinaigrette

WARM ASPARAGUS AND FOIE GRAS SALAD

TO SERVE 4:

24 medium asparagus spears
1 large shallot
1 sprig parsley
6 tablespoons wine vinegar
6 tablespoons walnut oil
Two ½-inch-thick slices raw duck foie gras, about 1¾ ounces
    each (see **NOTE**)
Salt and pepper
Flour, for coating the foie gras

PREPARATIONS:

Cut off the bottom of the asparagus stalks so that you have 4-inch spears and peel the stalk ends of these spears. Chop the shallot. Mince enough parsley to make ½ teaspoon.

FINISHING:

Cook the asparagus spears in salted boiling water for 10 minutes. Leave them in the hot water to keep warm until ready to assemble the salad. In a saucepan, cook the vinegar and the shallot for 1 minute over high heat, add the walnut oil, and remove the pan from the heat but cover it to keep warm.

Heat a non-stick frying pan over high heat. Salt and pepper the foie gras slices and flour them lightly. Sauté them very quickly, about 30 seconds on each side. Remove the slices from the pan and cut them into ⅛-inch-thick strips. Quickly drain the asparagus, cut a ½-inch slice from the end of each spear, and add these slices to the warm vinaigrette.

PRESENTATION:

Arrange the asparagus in fan shapes on warm plates, put the foie gras strips over them, and nap with the vinaigrette. Sprinkle with the parsley.

NOTE: *This recipe is celestial made with foie gras, but it is also a delicious way to use chicken livers. Use about ¼ pound of whole livers. Season and flour them as in the recipe and sauté in a non-stick pan with 2 teaspoons of oil for 2 minutes, turning once. See page 30 for information on raw foie gras. Ed.*

Foie gras de canard chaud en salade

WARM FOIE GRAS AND ARTICHOKE SALAD

TO SERVE 4:

1 onion
8 small violet artichokes (see **NOTES**)
1 tablespoon butter
¼ cup white wine
1 handful arugula (see **NOTES**)
¼ teaspoon mustard
1 tablespoon vinegar
2 tablespoons peanut oil
Salt and pepper
Four ½-inch slices raw duck foie gras, about 1¾ ounces each
    (see page 30)
Flour, for cooking the foie gras

PREPARATIONS:

Slice the onion. Remove the outside leaves and the stems from the artichokes and cook the artichokes, covered, with the onion, butter, and white wine about 20 minutes, or until they are tender. Add a bit of water if the wine evaporates. Chill until ready to assemble the salad. Wash and dry the arugula. Whisk together the mustard, vinegar, oil, and salt and pepper.

FINISHING AND PRESENTATION:

Cut each artichoke into 8 sections, dress them with some of the vinaigrette, and arrange 16 sections on each salad plate in a star design. Dress the arugula with the remaining vinaigrette and then put a quarter of it in the middle of each plate.

Heat a non-stick frying pan over high heat. Season the slices of foie gras, coat them lightly with flour, and cook them quickly, about 30 seconds on each side. Put a slice of foie gras in the middle of each plate, on top of the arugula, and serve immediately.

NOTES: *If the tiny violet artichokes are not available, use the smallest you can find. Cut into thin sections and remove chokes. Ed.*

Salade printanière
de caille au foie gras de canard

SPRINGTIME SALAD WITH QUAIL AND FOIE GRAS

TO SERVE 4:

2 quail
4 ounces (about 6 cups) dandelion or other spring greens
1 spring onion
1 tomato
1 sprig each chervil, parsley, and tarragon
1 blade chive
2 tablespoons wine vinegar
6 tablespoons walnut oil
Salt and pepper
A few drops peanut oil
3 tablespoons butter
7 ounces raw duck foie gras (see page 30)
Flour, for coating the foie gras

PREPARATIONS:

Cut up the quail in the following manner: Cut off the first two joints of the wing. Slice down the middle of the breast of each bird and then, keeping the blade against the bones to get all the meat, remove the flesh from one side and then the other, keeping the remaining wing pieces attached to the breasts. Now remove the legs, detaching them at the hip joint and then carefully divide into drumsticks and thighs. You can save the wing joints and the carcass to use in stock.

Wash and dry the dandelion leaves and put in a bowl. Slice the onion and add it to the bowl. Peel and seed the tomato and cut it into ¼-inch dice. Chop enough chervil, parsley, tarragon, and chive to make 1 teaspoon altogether. Whisk together the vinegar, walnut oil, and salt and pepper. Dress the tomato dice with a spoonful of this vinaigrette.

FINISHING AND PRESENTATION:

Salt and pepper the quail pieces. Put a non-stick frying pan over high heat. When it's hot, add a few drops of peanut oil and then sear the quail pieces in the nearly dry pan over high heat, skin side down. After a minute, turn the pieces and after another minute add the butter, lower the heat to medium, and cook the quail pieces 4 more minutes, turning them once or twice.

While the quail is cooking, toss the dandelion greens with some of the vinaigrette and divide them among four plates. Cut the foie gras into ½-inch dice. Remove the skin from the cooked quail pieces and slice the quail breasts lengthwise so that the slices of each breast can be fanned out around the wing bone. Put all the quail pieces in the vinaigrette for a minute and then arrange them on the plates with the greens. Wipe out the frying pan with paper towels.

Season the foie gras cubes and flour lightly. In the frying pan, sauté them over high heat for 1 minute, tossing or turning to brown all sides. The pan should not have any oil in it and should be very hot so that the foie gras will render its fat rapidly and form a crisp crust.

Remove the foie gras from the pan with a slotted spoon, dip the pieces in the remaining vinaigrette, and then scatter them over the salads. Top with the tomato and sprinkle with the herbs.

Salade de cuisses de
grenouilles aux fèves fraîches

FROG LEG AND FAVA BEAN SALAD

TO SERVE 4:

4½ pounds fava (or broad) beans in their shells, about 1⅔
    pounds or 4 cups shelled (see **NOTE** page 40)
3 ounces (about 3 slices) bacon
1 shallot
1 garlic clove
1 small onion
3 sprigs flat-leaf parsley
1½ to 2 pounds frog legs
Salt and pepper
¼ teaspoon flour
1 teaspoon heavy cream
5 tablespoons peanut oil, plus a few drops for sautéing
2 tablespoons butter
4 teaspoons red-wine vinegar

PREPARATIONS:

Shell the beans and cook them for 2 minutes in salted boiling water. Drain them, let them
cool a bit, and then remove their skins. Cut the bacon slices crosswise into thin julienne
strips, about ⅛ inch wide.

    Mince the shallot and garlic. Cut the onion into very thin slices. Mince enough pars-
ley to make 1 tablespoon. Bone the frog legs by slitting them along both sides and pulling
out the bones, making sure that you get all the meat from them.

FINISHING:

Fry the bacon until brown and drain on paper towels. Put the frog leg meat in a bowl,
season with salt and pepper, and dust with the flour. Add the cream and mix with your
hands. The meat should be coated with a sticky cream. Put a few drops of oil in a non-
stick pan and heat it over high heat. When the pan is quite hot, put the frog leg meat in
and stir with a wooden spatula. The pieces should separate from each other easily. In
about 1 minute, when they've started to brown, add the minced garlic and shallot and

the butter and finish cooking until they're nicely golden brown, 1 minute longer. Stir in the parsley and remove the pan from the heat.

Mix the beans, bacon strips, and sliced onion in a large bowl and dress with the red-wine vinegar, 5 tablespoons peanut oil, and salt and pepper.

PRESENTATION:

Put a fourth of the frog legs in the center of each of four plates and surround with the bean salad. Serve immediately.

Salade de perdrix
des neiges aux endives et cèpes

PARTRIDGE SALAD WITH ENDIVES AND CÈPES

TO SERVE 4:

4 snow partridges (see **COMMENT**)
2 Belgian endives
½ pound cèpes
2 shallots
½ lemon
1 tablespoon vinegar, plus a few drops for finishing
2 tablespoons walnut oil
Salt and pepper
2 tablespoons butter
3 sprigs dried thyme
¼ cup peanut oil

PREPARATIONS:

Cut off the wings of each bird. Slice down the middle of the breast of each bird and remove the suprêmes, cutting carefully with the blade against the bones to remove all the meat from each side of the breast. You will use only the suprêmes. (see **NOTE**.)

Cut the endives lengthwise into thin julienne strips. Clean the cèpes and cut them into thin slices. Chop the shallots. Squeeze the juice from the ½ lemon. Whisk together the vinegar, walnut oil, lemon juice, and salt and pepper to make a vinaigrette.

FINISHING:

Toss the endive strips with the vinaigrette.

In a frying pan, heat 1 tablespoon of the butter over medium heat. Season the su-prêmes and sauté them in the butter along with the sprigs of thyme. You only need to sauté them for 2 to 3 minutes. They should just firm up and still be red inside. Remove the suprêmes and set them aside.

In a frying pan, heat the peanut oil over high heat and add the cèpes. Cook them until their juices evaporate and they brown lightly and then add the remaining 1 tablespoon of butter and the chopped shallots. Season with salt and pepper. Continue cooking 1 minute and then remove from the heat and sprinkle with a few drops of vinegar.

PRESENTATION:

Serve the salad on heated plates. Arrange the endives in a fan shape at the top of each plate, put two pieces of partridge in the center, and the cèpes at the bottom.

COMMENT: The white partridges of the Alps, or snow partridges, are now nearly impossible to find. For this salad, substitute two 1-pound partridges or squabs.

NOTE: *The legs can be sautéed in the same manner as the suprêmes. Use the rest of the carcass for stock. Ed.*

Salade de ris de veau aux pois gourmands

SWEETBREAD SALAD WITH SNOW PEAS

TO SERVE 4:

2 lobes sweetbreads, about 1 pound in all (see **COMMENT**)
48 snow peas, about ½ pound
½ lime
2 teaspoons vinegar
Salt and pepper
2 teaspoons walnut oil
A few drops olive oil

PREPARATIONS:

Put the sweetbreads in a bowl and set under cold running water for 3 to 4 hours. Using a small knife, cut and peel away the membrane and fat. With a thin, sharp knife, cut the sweetbreads lengthwise into ¼-inch slices. You should have 12 to 16 slices.

String the peas, separate the pods, and discard any tiny peas inside. Cook the pods for 2 minutes in salted boiling water and drain them. Grate a pinch of lime zest into a bowl and then squeeze the juice from the lime over it. Add the vinegar and salt and pepper and whisk in the walnut oil to make a vinaigrette.

FINISHING:

Toss the snow pea pods in the vinaigrette. Salt and pepper the sweetbread slices. Heat a non-stick frying pan with a few drops of olive oil in it over high heat. Put in the sweetbread slices and sauté them for 1 minute on each side.

PRESENTATION:

Arrange about half the snow pea pods like rays of the sun in the center of each plate. Put a mound of the remaining pods in the middle and the sweetbread slices on top. Serve immediately.

COMMENT: The sweetbreads are not to be blanched before cooking.

entrées chaudes

WARM FIRST COURSES

Asperges à la mousseline d'huîtres

ASPARAGUS WITH OYSTER MOUSSELINE SAUCE

TO SERVE 4:

24 asparagus spears
8 oysters
¼ cup white wine
4 egg yolks
2 tablespoons heavy cream
Salt and pepper
1 pinch cayenne
3 tablespoons butter

PREPARATIONS:

Cut the asparagus stalks off so that you have 4-inch spears and peel the stalk ends of these spears. Open the oysters and save the liquor. If you buy shucked oysters, be sure to ask for their liquor so that you will have about ¼ cup. Cut the oysters into strips about ⅛ inch thick. Pour the oyster liquor through a cheesecloth-lined strainer into a small heavy saucepan, add the white wine, and reduce by two thirds by boiling over high heat.

Cook the asparagus spears 10 minutes in salted boiling water, remove from the heat, and leave in the hot water to keep warm.

Beat together the egg yolks, ½ cup of the water in which the asparagus has been cooked, and the cream. Pour this mixture into the pan with the white-wine and oyster-liquor reduction and put the saucepan over very low heat. Whisk until the mixture is very foamy and lightly thickened. Season with salt, pepper, and a pinch of cayenne and, with the saucepan still over low heat, whisk in the 3 tablespoons butter.

Now add the oyster strips to the sauce and immediately drain the asparagus and cut from the bottom of each spear two ¼-inch slices. Add the slices to the sauce.

PRESENTATION

Arrange the asparagus spears in fan shapes on warm plates and nap their tips with the oyster mousseline sauce.

PUFF PASTRY WITH ASPARAGUS AND FRESH TRUFFLES

TO SERVE 6:

3 eggs (see **COMMENT**)
30 asparagus spears
4 ounces fresh truffles (see **NOTES**)
1 shallot
4 tablespoons butter
Salt and pepper
1 ¾ pounds **puff pastry** (page 241)
2 egg yolks
1 ½ tablespoons each madeira and port
3 tablespoons truffle juice (see **NOTES**)
1 teaspoon meat juice, optional

PREPARATIONS:

Hard boil the eggs and slice into rounds. Cut the ends from the asparagus spears so that the tips are about 3 inches long and cook the tips in salted boiling water for about 2 minutes. Remove them while they are still quite firm and drain them.

Slice the truffles into rounds ⅛ inch thick. Chop the shallot and put it in a non-stick frying pan with 1 tablespoon of the butter. Heat until the butter melts and then add the truffle rounds. Salt and pepper them and sauté for 2 minutes over high heat. Remove the pan from the heat and set the truffles aside to cool in the pan.

On a lightly floured work surface, roll out a long puff-pastry strip 8 inches wide and 26 inches long. Cut it in two lengthwise to make one 8-by-12½-inch rectangle and one 8-by-13½-inch rectangle. With a fork, prick the pastry thoroughly, every ½ inch or so. If you are not going to bake the pastry immediately, put it back in the refrigerator to wait, protected with plastic wrap.

COOKING:

Heat the oven to 425°F. Place the shorter rectangle of pastry on a baking sheet. Arrange 15 of the asparagus spears in one layer down the middle of the pastry, tips all pointing the same way, leaving a wide border on all four sides. Salt and pepper the asparagus. Now put a layer of hard-boiled egg slices on top of the asparagus and salt lightly. Set aside a scant quarter of the truffles for the sauce and put the rest on the eggs, making sure that you don't brush the truffles against the pastry edges since this will keep them from sealing. Save the pan with the truffle cooking liquid. Put another layer of asparagus spears, tips facing in the opposite direction, on the truffles. Salt and pepper lightly.

Prepare a glaze by whisking the 2 egg yolks with a pinch of salt. Use a pastry brush to glaze the borders of the puff pastry. Top with the remaining piece of pastry and use your hands to shape and equalize the filling and then to press the puff-pastry sheets together all around the edges. Trim the edges with a knife so that the pastry border is about an inch wide all around the filling and then cut the corners off on the diagonal. Dip the tip end of a spoon handle in flour and use it to score the puff pastry with decorative semicircles and to seal it, pressing the handle down into the pastry edge at ⅛-inch intervals. You must push down on the spoon firmly and also push back into the pastry just a little to make a good seal.

Decorate the surface of the puff pastry by tracing shallow, parallel diagonal lines over the top with the point of a sharp knife. Brush the surface of the pastry with the glaze. Bake it in the preheated oven for 35 minutes. Watch to make sure it does not burn. When the puff pastry is done, transfer carefully to a platter.

Now chop the truffle slices set aside earlier. Put the pan with the cooking juices from the truffles back on the stove. When reheated, deglaze with the port and madeira mixture and boil to reduce by half. Now add the truffle juice and, if using, the meat juice. Put the chopped truffles in the pan and finish the sauce by swirling in the remaining 3 tablespoons of butter.

PRESENTATION:

Take the puff pastry and the sauce, in a sauceboat, to the table. Cut the puff pastry in slices and serve with a little of the sauce.

COMMENT: Perfume the eggs in their shells by putting them the day before in a tightly covered jar with the fresh truffles. This is well worth doing!

NOTES: *Morels made a good substitution for truffles in this recipe. Use ¾ to 1 cup fresh or ½ ounce (about ½ cup) dried, first soaked in warm water for at least half an hour.*

You may substitute additional meat juice, stock, or even asparagus cooking liquid for the truffle juice. If you use dried morels instead of truffles, use the strained soaking water instead of the truffle juice.

See page 31 for information on truffles and truffle juice. Ed.

Cassolette de truffes et cardons

TRUFFLES AND CARDOONS IN MADEIRA SAUCE

TO SERVE 4:

Eight 4-inch pieces cardoon (see **NOTE**)
2 tablespoons flour
2 cups water
½ lemon
1 tablespoon peanut oil
Salt and pepper
4 fresh truffles, about 1 ounce each (see page 31)
2 shallots
7 tablespoons butter
½ cup madeira
½ cup **chicken stock** (page 232)
¼ cup **veal stock** (page 234)

PREPARATIONS:

Pluck the outer leaves from the cardoon pieces and remove the strings. Cut the cardoons into ¼-inch slices. Put the flour in a saucepan and gradually add the water, whisking. Squeeze in 1 tablespoon lemon juice. Add the oil and salt and bring to a boil. Add the cardoons and cook until tender, about 30 minutes. Drain and set aside.

Mince the shallots. Slice the truffles into rounds about ⅛ inch thick.

FINISHING:

Put the shallots, 4 tablespoons of the butter, and the truffle slices in a saucepan. Heat until the butter foams, remove the pan from the heat, cover it, and put it back over a very, very low heat for 2 more minutes. Now add the madeira, chicken stock, and veal stock to the pan, let simmer, still over low heat and with the cover on, for 4 minutes.

Add the cardoon slices to the pan, season them with salt and pepper, thin the sauce if necessary with a small spoonful of water, and then reheat over low heat. Finally swirl the remaining 3 tablespoons of butter into the sauce.

If possible serve these in small individual pans or casseroles with covers so that each person can appreciate the perfume of the truffle when the lid is removed.

NOTE: *The cardoon is an edible Mediterranean thistle related to the artichoke. It is rarely found in the United States outside of home gardens. Chef Girardet suggests substituting salsify in this recipe, cooked by the same method. Or he suggests asparagus, cooked until just done in plain salted boiling water. Ed.*

Escalope de foie gras
de canard à la vinaigrette

FOIE GRAS IN WARM VINAIGRETTE

TO SERVE 4:

1 shallot
1 sprig each chervil and parsley
3 blades chives
2½ tablespoons wine vinegar
Salt and pepper
2½ tablespoons walnut oil
Four ½-inch slices raw duck foie gras, about 7 ounces in all (see page 30)
Flour, for coating the foie gras

PREPARATIONS:

Mince the shallot. Chop enough of the herbs together to make 1 tablespoon in all.

FINISHING:

Cook the vinegar, shallot, and salt and pepper in a small saucepan over medium-high heat for 1 minute. Add the walnut oil, remove from the heat, and keep warm. Salt and pepper each slice of foie gras and flour it lightly. Heat a non-stick pan over high heat and when it is hot sauté the foie gras slices in it, without any oil, for 30 seconds on each side. Add the mixed herbs to the warm vinaigrette.

PRESENTATION:

Put the foie gras on small warm plates and nap with the vinaigrette. Serve immediately.

Tarte à l'oignon

ONION TART

TO SERVE 6 TO 8:

Pastry:

1 ½ cups flour
¼ pound (1 stick) butter, softened
1 pinch salt
1 egg

Filling:

¾ pound (2 to 3) onions
1 ounce (about 1 slice) bacon
3 tablespoons butter
3 sprigs parsley
1 cup heavy cream
1 cup milk
4 eggs
½ teaspoon salt, or to taste
Pepper
Nutmeg

PREPARATIONS:

To make the pastry, in a bowl work the flour, butter, and salt together with your fingertips until the mixture is the consistency of meal. Stir in the egg and then add 2 to 4 tablespoons water, a tablespoon at a time, until the dough can be pressed together into a ball. The amount of water needed depends on the flour used. Refrigerate the dough.

Cut the onions into thin slices. Cut the bacon crosswise into thin julienne strips. In a frying pan over low heat, brown the bacon in the 3 tablespoons butter. Add the sliced onions and cook until tender.

Mince the parsley. In a bowl, whisk together the cream, milk, and eggs and add the salt, pepper, and a few gratings nutmeg to taste. When the onions are tender, add them to this mixture and stir in the minced parsley.

Butter a 10-inch tart pan. Roll out the dough on a lightly floured surface until it is very thin and large enough to fit the pan. Line the pan with the pastry and push up the edge so that it extends above the rim of the pan. Prick the bottom with a fork. Cut a disk of aluminum foil to fit the base of the pan and put it on top of the dough.

COOKING:

Heat the oven to 325°F. Bake the pastry for 30 minutes without letting any of the crust except the edges color. When the edges have browned lightly, remove the tart shell from the oven, take out the aluminum foil, and add the onion filling. Return the tart to the oven and turn off the oven. Let the tart bake with the heat turned off for 1 hour.

COMMENT: Each time we've tried to serve a different hors d'oeuvre with apéritifs, our clients have demanded the return of the onion tart.

Feuilleté au lapin et basilic

RABBIT WITH BASIL IN PUFF PASTRY

TO SERVE 4:

½ pound **puff pastry** (page 241)
1 or 2 rabbit hind legs, to yield about ½ pound boned meat
1 pound fava (or broad) beans in their pods, about 5 ounces or
    ¼ cup shelled (see **NOTES** page 40)
12 leaves fresh basil
1 shallot
Salt and pepper
2 tablespoons butter
⅔ cup heavy cream

PREPARATIONS:

Heat the oven to 425°F. Roll out the puff pastry and cut it into 4 rectangles, each about 3½ by 2½ inches. Turn them over and put on a baking sheet. (Refrigerate if not baking immediately.) Bake the puff pastry for 10 minutes. Reduce the heat to 375°F and bake for 15 to 20 minutes longer, until thoroughly cooked.

Bone the rabbit legs and remove the tendons. You should have about ½ pound of meat. Slice the meat into pieces about ¼ inch thick, 2 inches long, and ¾ inch wide and set aside on a plate.

Remove the fava beans from their pods. Cook the beans in salted boiling water for 2 minutes. Drain them, remove their skins, and set them aside. Cut the basil leaves into fine strips and mince the shallot.

FINISHING:

Heat the oven to 350°F. Slice the puff-pastry rectangles in two horizontally, cutting about one third of the way down from the top, and put them in the oven to reheat.

Reserve any juices that have accumulated from the raw rabbit and season the slices with salt and pepper. Melt the butter over low heat in a frying pan. When it starts to foam, put the rabbit slices in the pan along with the shallot and stir for about 1½ minutes. When the meat turns white on the outside, remove and set aside. Add the cream to the frying pan, increase the heat so that the cream boils, and reduce it for 2 minutes. Now put the basil and beans in the pan, salt and pepper the sauce, and bring it to a boil two or three times so that the beans are reheated.

Remove the puff pastry from the oven and raise the heat to 400°F. Remove the beans from the frying pan with a slotted spoon and put ¼ of them on the bottom part of each puff pastry. Arrange the rabbit slices on top of the beans and then cover with the puff-pastry tops. Put the filled pastries in the preheated oven for 1 minute. Add the rabbit juice set aside earlier to the sauce, check the seasoning, and if the sauce is too thick, add water by teaspoons to thin it.

PRESENTATION:

Put the pastries on individual plates and pour the sauce around them.

COMMENT: This is the kind of recipe you discover when racking your brain to try to please your accountant . . . and because rabbits have legs.

Feuilleté au foie
de lapin et aux poireaux

RABBIT LIVER AND LEEKS IN PUFF PASTRY

TO SERVE 4:

½ pound **puff pastry** (page 241)
2 leeks
2 rabbit livers
6 tablespoons butter
3 tablespoons water
⅓ cup heavy cream
Salt and pepper

PREPARATIONS:

Heat the oven to 425°F. Roll out the puff pastry and cut it into 4 rectangles, each about 3½ by 2½ inches. Turn them over and put on a baking sheet. (Refrigerate if not baking immediately.) Bake the puff pastry for 10 minutes. Reduce the heat to 375°F and bake for 15 to 20 minutes longer, until thoroughly cooked.

Use only the white and light-green parts of the leeks. Cut off and discard the dark green leaves. Wash the leeks. Cut them lengthwise into quarters and then into slices about ½ inch thick. Separate the layers. Cut the livers crosswise into slices about ¼ inch thick.

FINISHING:

Heat the oven to 350°F. Slice the puff-pastry rectangles in two horizontally, cutting about one third of the way down from the top, and put them in the oven to reheat.

Brown the leeks quickly in a frying pan with 2 tablespoons of the butter. Add the water and cook over low heat until the water completely evaporates. Add the cream, cook over high heat for 1 minute, season with salt and pepper, remove from the heat, and add 2 tablespoons of the butter. Set aside and keep warm.

Season the sliced rabbit livers. Heat another frying pan over high heat until it is quite hot and then add the remaining 2 tablespoons of butter. When the butter foam dies down, add the liver slices, sauté them for 20 seconds, and season with salt and pepper.

Remove the puff pastry from the oven and raise the heat to 400°F. Spread some of the leeks on the bottom part of each pastry, using about half of them in all. Arrange the rabbit livers over the leeks and top with the rest of the leeks. Cover with the puff-pastry tops and set the filled pastries in the preheated oven for 1 minute.

PRESENTATION:

Put the pastries on warm plates and serve immediately.

Béatilles de lapin
aux morilles et truffes noires

RABBIT TIDBITS WITH MORELS AND BLACK TRUFFLES

TO SERVE 4:

2 rabbit livers (see **COMMENTS**)
4 rabbit kidneys (see **COMMENTS**)
¼ pound morels
1½ ounces fresh truffles (see **NOTES**)
1 shallot
½ spring onion (see page 31)
1 sprig parsley
6 tablespoons butter
2 tablespoons madeira
2 tablespoons port
2 tablespoons truffle juice, optional
Salt and pepper
A few drops peanut oil

PREPARATIONS:

Cut the livers and kidneys into ⅛-inch slices. Wash the morels carefully and cut them in half lengthwise. Cut the truffles into ⅛-inch slices. Mince the shallot and cut the onion into thin slices. Chop enough parsley to make ½ teaspoon.

FINISHING:

Put 2 tablespoons of the butter, the truffles, and the shallot into a small heavy saucepan. Put it over high heat for 2 minutes and then add the madeira, port, and the truffle juice, if using, or 2 tablespoons stock or water. Bring to a boil, scraping the bottom of the pan with a wooden spatula. Season with salt and pepper and keep warm.

Heat 2 tablespoons of the butter in a frying pan, add the morels, and let them brown over medium heat until all their rendered juices have evaporated. Season them with salt and pepper and add the sliced onion. Set aside.

Salt and pepper the rabbit liver and kidney slices. Heat the oil in a frying pan over high heat. Add the liver and kidney slices, sauté them 20 seconds, add 1 tablespoon of the butter, cook another 20 seconds, and then remove from the heat. Over medium heat, finish the sauce by swirling the remaining tablespoon of butter into the pan with the truffles and then adding the morels.

PRESENTATION:

Put the sauce in cassolettes (small individual pans), or in ramekins or whatever small, attractive dishes you have. Arrange the livers and kidneys on top of the sauce and sprinkle with the chopped parsley.

COMMENTS: If you want to serve this as a main dish, double the amounts. The same dish can be made with veal; for a first course, use 4 ounces veal liver and 4 ounces veal kidney.

NOTES: *If you wish to make this dish without truffles, increase the quantity of fresh morels to ⅓ pound.*

See page 31 for information on truffles. Ed.

TRUFFLE RAVIOLI

TO SERVE 2 TO 4:

⅓ pound **ravioli dough** (page 240)
3¾ ounces (about 1½ bunches) parsley
1 ounce fresh truffles (see page 31)
½ shallot
4½ tablespoons butter
Salt and pepper
1 egg yolk
¼ cup truffle juice (see **NOTE**)

PREPARATIONS:

Prepare the ravioli dough and let it rest in the refrigerator, covered with plastic wrap, for 30 minutes.

Cut or twist the large stems off the parsley and discard or save for bouquet garni. Blanch the parsley leaves in a pan of salted boiling water for 1 minute. Drain the parsley, refresh it in cold water, and then drain it well. Squeeze dry by handfuls and spread on paper towels.

Chop the truffles and mince the shallot. Chop the well-dried parsley. In a small saucepan, put 1 tablespoon of the butter and the minced shallot and cook over high heat until the butter starts to foam. Reduce heat to low, add the chopped truffles and salt and pepper, and cook over low heat for 2 minutes, stirring. Remove from the heat, add the parsley, and mix well. Check the seasoning and set this filling aside to cool before using.

Roll out the ravioli dough to a rectangle that is at least 10 by 20 inches and nearly transparent. It will be difficult to do this with a rolling pin. You will probably need a pasta machine, which should be set on the thinnest possible setting. Since the dough has a tendency to stick, you should flour it lightly before rolling it out.

Divide the thinly rolled pasta in half. In a small bowl, beat the egg yolk and ¾ teaspoon water with a fork until combined. Brush 1 sheet of the pasta thoroughly with this glaze. Divide the parsley and truffle filling, making 16 little mounds at regular intervals on the glazed pasta sheet. Drape the other sheet of pasta over them. Press with your fingers around the mounds of filling to seal and push out the air bubbles from between the layers. Use a scalloped ravioli cutter 2 inches in diameter to cut the 16 ravioli.

FINISHING:

Bring a pot of salted water to a boil. In a medium-size saucepan, melt 1 ½ tablespoons of the butter and let cool to lukewarm while you cook the ravioli in the boiling water for 3 minutes. Drain the ravioli, put them immediately into the saucepan with the warm butter, and toss gently. In a small heavy saucepan, bring the truffle juice to a full boil. Remove from the heat and swirl in the remaining 2 tablespoons of butter to make a lightly thickened sauce. Check the seasoning.

PRESENTATION:

Serve the ravioli on warm plates, either four or eight ravioli per person depending on the menu. Pour the sauce over the ravioli.

NOTE: *See page 31 for information on truffles and truffle juice. For truffle juice, you can substitute another liquid such as stock or a combination of half madeira and half water. Ed.*

poissons

F I S H

NOTE: *The recipes in this chapter are designed as fish courses, almost all to serve four people, before the main course. It is necessary to check the amounts of the principal ingredients first, but you will find that they are usually appropriate to serve two as a main course. Ed.*

Suprême de loup
au céleri-rave et au vinaigre

STRIPED BASS WITH CELERY ROOT AND VINEGAR

TO SERVE 4:

¾ to 1 pound striped bass fillets (see **NOTE**)
2 shallots
⅓ cup vinegar
¼ cup port
1 small tomato
3 sprigs each chervil and parsley
1 small celery root, about ½ pound
2 tablespoons white wine
Salt and pepper
12 tablespoons (1 ½ sticks) butter, plus butter for the baking dish
1 tablespoon peanut oil

PREPARATIONS:

Cut the fillets diagonally so that you have 4 pieces of about equal size. Put them between pieces of waxed paper and pound lightly with the flat of a cleaver or with a rolling pin to flatten them slightly and to even the thickness.

Mince the shallots. Put them in a small heavy pan with the vinegar and reduce by two thirds over medium heat. Add the port and set aside. Peel and seed the tomato and cut it into small dice. Chop enough chervil and parsley to make 1 tablespoon of each. Peel the celery root and cut it into ¼-inch cubes.

Arrange the fillets in a buttered metal platter or baking dish and sprinkle them with the white wine. Salt and pepper the fish and dot the fillets with 1 tablespoon of the butter.

FINISHING:

Heat the oven to 525°F. Bake the fish, turning the fillets over once, for 1 ½ to 2 minutes per side, depending on the thickness of the fillets. Remove and keep them warm. Meanwhile, heat the oil in a frying pan over high heat, add the celery root, and sauté quickly until it browns, 3 to 4 minutes. Season with salt and pepper and add 1 tablespoon of the butter to the pan. Remove the pan from the heat.

Bring the shallot and vinegar reduction to a boil, reduce the heat to very low, and then whisk in the remaining 10 tablespoons of butter a bit at a time to make a lightly thickened sauce. Add the tomato dice and the chervil and season with salt and pepper.

PRESENTATION:

Put one fillet in the center of each plate with a mound of celery root next to it. Surround with the sauce and sprinkle with the parsley.

NOTE: *The closest American equivalent to loup is striped bass, which is an excellent substitute since it is notable in its texture and flavor. Black sea bass and red snapper are other possible substitutes. Ed.*

Escalope de loup aux huîtres

STRIPED BASS WITH OYSTERS

TO SERVE 4:

¾ pound striped bass fillets (see **NOTE**, preceding recipe)
12 oysters
⅓ cup white wine, plus a few drops
Salt and pepper
1 pinch cayenne
⅓ cup heavy cream
4 tablespoons butter, plus butter for the baking dish
Chervil leaves, for garnish

PREPARATIONS:

Cut the fillets diagonally so that you have 4 pieces of about equal size. Put them between pieces of waxed paper and pound lightly with the flat of a cleaver or with a rolling pin to flatten them slightly and to even the thickness.

Open the oysters and pour their liquor through a cheesecloth-lined strainer into a small heavy saucepan. If you buy shucked oysters, be sure to have them packed with their liquor. Add the wine to the oyster liquor and reduce the mixture over high heat to about 2 tablespoons. Arrange the bass fillets on a buttered metal platter or baking dish, season with salt and pepper and a pinch of cayenne, and then trickle a few drops of white wine on the fish.

FINISHING:

Heat the oven to 525°F. Add the cream to the pan with the reduced oyster-liquor and white-wine mixture, bring to a boil, and then reduce the heat to low. Whisk in the butter, a bit at a time, to make a lightly thickened sauce. Remove from the heat, check for seasoning, and immediately put the oysters into the sauce, still off the heat, to let them just barely cook. Bake the fillets in the preheated oven, turning them over once, for 1½ minutes per side.

PRESENTATION:

Serve on warm plates, each piece of bass fillet topped with three oysters, coated with sauce, and garnished with a few leaves of chervil.

Escalope de loup aux artichauts

STRIPED BASS WITH ARTICHOKES

TO SERVE 4:

2 cooked **artichoke bottoms** (page 239)
10 ounces striped bass fillets (see **NOTE** page 86)
4 large or 8 small lobsterettes (see **NOTE**)
1 small red pepper
6 leaves fresh basil
Salt and pepper
A few drops white wine
4 tablespoons butter, plus extra for the baking dish
½ cup heavy cream

PREPARATIONS:

Prepare the artichokes and cut each bottom into 6 sections. Keep 4 tablespoons of the cooking liquid for the sauce.

Cut the fillets diagonally so that you have 4 pieces of about equal size. Put them between pieces of waxed paper and pound lightly with the flat of a cleaver or with a rolling pin to flatten them slightly and to even the thickness. Twist off the lobsterette tails and remove the meat from the tail sections by cutting the ribbed underside with scissors and pulling away the shell so that the meat emerges in one piece.

Blanch the red pepper in boiling water for 5 minutes and peel it. Remove the seeds and the white parts of the pepper and cut it into fine julienne strips. Cut the basil leaves into fine strips. Butter a metal platter or shallow baking dish, put the bass pieces on it, season them with salt and pepper, and sprinkle a few drops of white wine on them. Dot the fish with 1 tablespoon of the butter.

FINISHING:

Heat the oven to 525°F. Start the sauce by reducing 4 tablespoons of the artichoke cooking liquid and the ½ cup of cream in a heavy saucepan over high heat. When it has reduced by half, turn the heat to low and whisk the remaining 3 tablespoons of butter into it. Add the pepper and artichokes and warm them over very low heat so that the vegetables warm but the sauce does not melt further. Just before serving, add the basil and check the seasoning.

Put the fish in the preheated oven. It should cook 3 minutes in all. After 1 minute, add the lobsterette tails to the platter and turn the pieces of fish. (**COMMENT**: The cooking time is for the large lobsterette tails. Simply heat smaller ones in the sauce at the same time you add the pepper and artichokes. Or they can be sautéed over high heat for about 30 seconds. The lobsterettes are done when the flesh is firm.)

PRESENTATION:

Serve on warm plates. Garnish each bass fillet with a lobsterette tail and spoon the vegetables and sauce over the fish.

NOTE: *You can substitute the meat from a raw lobster tail, weighing 8 ounces in the shell, shelled and cut into ½-inch slices, for the lobsterettes. See page 31 for more information on lobsterettes. Ed.*

GOATFISH FILLETS WITH HERBS

TO SERVE 4:

1 small shallot
1 garlic clove
A bouquet of seasonal herbs such as chervil, parsley, tarragon, and chives
1 tomato
3 tablespoons olive oil
1 ½ tablespoons butter
4 goatfish fillets, about ⅔ pound in all (see **NOTE**)
Salt, pepper, and cayenne
½ cup white wine

PREPARATIONS:

Chop the shallot and garlic. Mince enough herbs to make ¼ cup. Peel and seed the tomato and cut the flesh into ⅛-inch dice.

Put the oil in a flameproof baking dish large enough to hold the fillets in one layer. Add the butter and melt over low heat. Salt and pepper the fish and sprinkle very lightly with cayenne. Arrange the fillets in the baking dish, sprinkle the garlic and shallot over them, and add the white wine.

FINISHING:

Heat the oven to 525°F. Cook the fish in the oven for 2 minutes, turn the fillets, and continue cooking for 1 minute more. Remove the fillets to warm plates. Put the baking dish over medium heat and add the herbs and diced tomato. Check the seasoning and bring to a boil.

PRESENTATION:

Pour the tomato-herb sauce around the fillets and serve.

NOTE: *Rouget, a red-skinned fish with delicate meat, is famous in Mediterranean cuisine. It is similar to the goatfish found around the Bahamas and the Florida Keys. About 100,000 pounds of goatfish per year are normally available in New York fish markets—a relatively small quantity. Where available the Hawaiian moano or kumo goatfish are recommended. Red snapper is a good substitute. Ed.*

Filets de rouget à la crème de romarin

GOATFISH FILLETS WITH ROSEMARY CREAM SAUCE

TO SERVE 4:

Four ⅓- to ½-pound goatfish (see **NOTE**, preceding recipe)
2 shallots
3 tablespoons butter
5 sprigs rosemary
⅓ cup white wine
⅓ cup water
½ cup heavy cream
Salt and pepper
¼ lemon
2 tablespoons peanut oil

PREPARATIONS:

Remove the fillets from the goatfish. You can ask your fish dealer to do this, but make sure you also get the livers (if using goatfish) and the bones and head. If you are especially sensitive to fish bones, use tweezers to remove the very fine bones found on the inside of the fillets. You can feel them when you run a finger down the fillet. Chop the goatfish livers into very small pieces. Chop the shallots.

In a saucepan, melt 2 tablespoons of the butter over medium heat. Add the bones and heads of the fish, break them into pieces with a wooden spatula, and let them cook for 1 or 2 minutes, stirring. Add the chopped shallots, cook for 2 minutes, and then add a large rosemary sprig broken into pieces. Now add the white wine and the water, reduce the heat to low, and let cook for 5 minutes. Strain this fumet and then pour it into a saucepan and reduce it over high heat by half.

FINISHING:

Reheat the reduced fumet, if necessary. Add the cream and boil to reduce until the sauce lightly coats the back of a spoon. Remove the pan from the heat and whisk in the remaining 1 tablespoon of butter. Add the goatfish livers and season the sauce with salt, pepper, and a touch of lemon juice. Keep warm.

Heat 1 tablespoon oil in each of two non-stick frying pans over medium-high heat and put 4 fillets in each, skin side down. Season and turn the fillets after 30 seconds, season the second side, and let them cook another 30 seconds.

PRESENTATION:

Pour the sauce onto warm plates. Put the fillets on top of the sauce and garnish each with a small rosemary sprig.

Saint-Pierre aux deux sauces

JOHN DORY WITH TWO SAUCES

TO SERVE 4:

2 shallots
1 branch tarragon
7 tablespoons butter
1 cup light red wine such as Fleurie, Brouilly, or Beaujolais-
    Villages
3 tablespoons **fish stock** (page 229)
1 teaspoon sugar
⅓ cup white wine
2 egg yolks
3 tablespoons heavy cream
Salt, pepper, and cayenne
1 pound John Dory fillets (see **NOTE**)
A few drops peanut oil

PREPARATIONS:

Chop the shallots. Chop enough tarragon to make ¼ teaspoon. In a small saucepan, melt 1 tablespoon of the butter and brown half the shallots. Add the red wine, the fish stock, and the sugar and reduce by one quarter. Remove from the heat and set aside. Put the white wine in a small heavy saucepan, add the rest of the shallots, and boil to reduce by half. Set aside.

FINISHING:

Whisk together the egg yolks and the cream, add to the reduced white wine and shallots, and whisk over very low heat. The heat should always be low enough so that you can put your hand on the bottom of the pan without burning your skin. Whisk until the mixture begins to thicken and then whisk in 3 tablespoons of the butter. Season with salt, pepper, and cayenne, and half the chopped tarragon.

While completing this mousseline sauce, reheat the red-wine reduction over low heat, whisk the remaining 3 tablespoons of butter into it, and season with salt and pepper. Season the fish fillets with salt and pepper. Heat the oil in a non-stick pan over high heat and then cook the fillets in the pan for 1 ½ minutes on each side.

PRESENTATION:

Serve the fish on warm plates. Put the red-wine sauce on each plate and a fillet in the middle of the plate. Mask each fillet with white-wine mousseline sauce and sprinkle with the rest of the tarragon.

NOTE: *John Dory is a firm, white-fleshed fish. It can be found off the American Atlantic coast but is rarely fished commercially. Bass and red snapper are good substitutes. Ed.*

Aiguillettes de Saint-Pierre au
confit d'oignons et au beurre de tomates

JOHN DORY WITH ONION COMPOTE AND TOMATO BUTTER

TO SERVE 4:

⅔ pound (2 to 3) onions
3 tablespoons red-wine vinegar, plus a few drops for finishing
1 cup red wine
1 cup water
4 teaspoons honey
8 tablespoons butter
Salt and pepper
3 tomatoes
1 pound John Dory fillets (see **NOTE,** preceding recipe)
⅛ teaspoon cayenne
A few drops peanut oil

PREPARATIONS:

Slice the onions. Put them in a saucepan with the 3 tablespoons vinegar and the red wine so that they're just covered with liquid. Cook them, uncovered, over low heat until they completely absorb the liquid, about 30 to 45 minutes. Now add the water to the pan and continue cooking, still over low heat, for another 30 minutes, or until the onions are very soft. Check occasionally to see that they do not stick to the bottom of the pan. Now add the honey and 2 tablespoons of the butter, season with salt and pepper, and set aside.

Core 2 of the tomatoes and cut in quarters without peeling. Whir the quarters in a food processor. Strain the resultant juice into a pan and cook it over medium heat until it is reduced by two thirds, to about ⅓ cup thick sauce. Remove from heat and set aside.

Separate each fillet into 2 strips following the natural divisions in the flesh. Peel the third tomato, remove the seeds, and cut the flesh into ⅛-inch dice.

FINISHING:

Reheat the onion compote, add a few drops vinegar, check the seasoning, and keep warm. Reheat the tomato sauce, whisk in the remaining 6 tablespoons of butter, and season with salt, pepper, and the cayenne. Stir in the tomato dice. Season the John Dory strips with salt and pepper and cook them for 1 ½ minutes per side on a grill or over high heat in a non-stick frying pan with a few drops of oil.

PRESENTATION:

Serve on heated plates. Put a quarter of the onion compote in the middle of each plate, place a strip of John Dory on it, and surround with the tomato butter.

COMMENT: This is a dish that pleased my friend Michel Guérard very much.

Ragoût de lotte au safran

MONKFISH STEW WITH SAFFRON

TO SERVE 4:

¾ pound boneless monkfish
⅓ pound boneless salmon
3 garlic cloves
4 leaves fresh basil
About ¼ pound little peas in their shells, to yield 2 tablespoons
    shelled
½ pound fava (or broad) beans in their shells, about 2 ½ ounces
    or 2 tablespoons shelled (see **NOTE** page 40)
1 ½ tablespoons olive oil
3 pinches powdered saffron
3 tablespoons **vegetable bouillon** (page 228)
½ cup heavy cream
1 pinch saffron threads
¼ lemon
Salt and pepper

PREPARATIONS:

Cut the monkfish once lengthwise and then five times crosswise to make 12 pieces each about 1 ½ inches by 1 ¼ inches. Cut the salmon into ½-inch cubes. Mince the garlic. Cut the basil leaves into thin strips. Shell the peas and beans and cook the peas for 10 minutes in boiling salted water. After 8 minutes, add the beans. Drain. Remove the skins from the beans.

FINISHING:

Put 1 tablespoon of the olive oil in a small saucepan over medium heat, add the garlic and 1 pinch of the powdered saffron, and cook 3 minutes. Add the vegetable bouillon, the cream, and the pinch of saffron threads and continue to cook, barely boiling, for 2 minutes. Check the seasoning and squeeze in lemon juice to taste, about 1 ½ teaspoons. Add the fava beans and the little peas and keep warm over very low heat.

In a non-stick pan, heat the remaining ½ tablespoon olive oil over high heat. Season the monkfish and the salmon with salt, pepper, and 2 pinches powdered saffron. Sauté the monkfish for 3 minutes. Remove the monkfish to warm plates and sauté the salmon, stirring constantly, for 30 seconds.

PRESENTATION:

On warm plates arrange the salmon around the monkfish. Nap the fish with the saffron sauce and sprinkle each serving with some basil strips.

SALMON WITH PISTOU AND TOMATO SAUCE

TO SERVE 4:

2 spring onions (see page 31)
4 tomatoes
⅓ cup water
6 garlic cloves
36 leaves fresh basil
6 tablespoons olive oil
Salt, pepper, and cayenne
2 salmon steaks about 1 inch thick, or 4 slices ½ inch thick
1 tablespoon butter
2 sprigs fresh thyme

PREPARATIONS:

Slice the spring onions and quarter the tomatoes. Put them in a saucepan over medium heat and add the water. Cook, uncovered, stirring occasionally, until all the tomatoes are very soft, 15 to 20 minutes. Strain into a bowl, pushing and scraping with a spoon to get all the tomato pulp. It should be thin enough to spread over a plate, but if it's too watery, reduce by boiling.

Peel the garlic, split the cloves, and discard the center germ of each one. Put the basil, the garlic, 5 tablespoons of the olive oil, and salt and pepper in the food processor. Whir until the basil and garlic are puréed. This is a classic Mediterranean pistou. Set aside.

Remove the skin from the salmon steaks, if necessary, and remove the bones. You should have ½ pound of fish. Cut 1-inch steaks in half horizontally. Rub the remaining tablespoon olive oil on a baking dish and arrange the 4 salmon slices on it. Season them with salt, pepper, and cayenne and put a quarter of the butter on each. Chop enough thyme to make 1 teaspoon.

FINISHING:

Heat the oven to 400°F. Cook the salmon in the oven for 2 minutes and then remove. It will finish cooking outside the oven while you arrange the pistou and sauce.

Reheat the tomato sauce, season it with salt and pepper, cayenne, and the thyme, and bring it just to a boil. The pistou can be served warm or at room temperature. To heat it, whisk it over low heat until it's lukewarm.

PRESENTATION:

Cover each plate with tomato sauce and put a slice of salmon in the middle. Mask the salmon with the pistou.

COMMENT: You can also serve this dish cold in the summer. Simply poach the salmon instead of cooking it in the oven and cool to room temperature.

Saumon en papillote au citron vert

SALMON PAPILLOTES WITH LIME SAUCE

TO SERVE 2:

1 salmon fillet (about ¾ pound) cut from the center
2 ½ tablespoons butter
Salt and pepper
1 pinch cayenne
Scant ½ teaspoon grated fresh ginger root, optional
1 lime
1 small shallot
1 ½ tablespoons port, plus a few drops for finishing
1 ½ tablespoons heavy cream

PREPARATIONS:

Lay the salmon fillet on a work surface and, holding your hand flat on the top of the fillet, cut it in half horizontally with a thin sharp knife. Cut 2 feet from a roll of 15-inch-wide sulfurized paper. Round off the corners to make an oval about 24 inches by 15 inches. Fold it in half crosswise and open it again. Butter half the paper from the fold to within 1 ½ inches of the edge, using 1 teaspoon of the butter; this will become the (inside) bottom of the papillote. Put the salmon slices side by side on the buttered part of the paper and season them with salt, pepper, a small pinch of cayenne, and, if you wish, ¼ teaspoon of the grated ginger. Now grate the zest from ¼ of the lime over them and sprinkle a few drops of lime juice on each salmon slice. Fold the sulfurized paper over the fish. Don't let the paper stick to the top of the fish and try to enclose as much air as possible when you seal the papillote. Roll up the edges and then press flat, making a sealed hem. Put the papillote on a large metal platter and set aside.

Chop the shallot and squeeze 2 tablespoons lime juice from the lime. In a small pan, soften the chopped shallot by cooking without browning in 2 teaspoons of the butter over low heat. Add the lime juice and port to the pan and over high heat reduce them by about half.

FINISHING:

Heat the oven to 525°F. The final preparation of the sauce and cooking of the salmon should be managed so that neither sauce nor papillote must wait for the other. But since both demand attention, it may be better not to try to do them simultaneously. In this case, finish the sauce first and then proceed immediately to cook the salmon. If the papillote is kept waiting, it will collapse.

To finish the sauce, reheat the reduced port and lime mixture, add the cream, and bring to a boil. Now, over very low heat, whisk into the sauce the remaining 1 ½ table-spoons of butter. Season with salt, pepper, a small pinch of cayenne, and just before serving, a few drops of port and, optionally, a little grated ginger. Put the metal platter with the papillote in the preheated oven and bake 3 minutes. It will inflate.

PRESENTATION:

Rush the papillote to the table along with the sauce in a sauceboat. Open the papillote at the table, put the salmon on plates, and nap with the lime sauce.

Brochette de saumon
et écrevisses à la menthe

SALMON AND CRAYFISH BROCHETTES WITH MINT

TO SERVE 4:

16 crayfish (see page 31)
1 carrot
1 onion
1 garlic clove
1 tablespoon olive oil
About 2 cups white wine
2 sprigs parsley
1 sprig thyme
1 branch rosemary
1 pound fava (or broad) beans in their shells, about 5 ounces or
    ¼ cup shelled (see **NOTE** page 40)
3 ounces (about 1 cup) snow peas
⅓ pound salmon fillet
6 mint leaves
4 tablespoons butter
Salt and pepper

PREPARATIONS:

Put the crayfish in a large pan of boiling water. After 1 minute, remove the crayfish, drain them, and let them cool a bit. Twist off each tail. Hold with both hands, top side down, with thumbs positioned along each side of the tail. Push to crack open and then remove the meat. Save the shells. Remove the vein from the tail meat, if you like, by pulling it out gently.

In a food processor or large mortar with pestle, crush the body and tail shells to release all the juices. Some chunks of shell are inevitable. Chop the carrot, onion, and garlic. Put the olive oil in a large saucepan over high heat and add the crushed crayfish shells and the chopped vegetables. Stir while the vegetables brown and then continue cooking until all the water released by the shells and vegetables has evaporated. Add enough white wine to barely cover the mixture and put in the parsley, thyme, and rosemary. Cook gently over low heat, uncovered, for 1 hour. Stir occasionally and check to make sure there's enough liquid. There should be at least ⅓ cup at the end; add water if necessary. When the stock is finished, put it through a fine strainer and set aside ⅓ cup in a small saucepan.

Shell the fava beans. Bring a pan of salted water to a boil and plunge the shelled beans into it. Let it come to a boil again and then cook for 2 minutes. Drain the beans and remove the skins. Set aside.

Remove the strings from the snow peas and cook them as you did the fava beans for 2 minutes in salted boiling water. Drain them and then cut them crosswise into squares.

Cut the salmon fillet into 20 pieces about ½ inch thick, ½ inch wide, and ¾ inch long. String the salmon pieces and crayfish onto four small skewers, alternating salmon and crayfish, and lining them up so that you have two flat sides. Cut the mint leaves into thin strips.

FINISHING:

Put the small saucepan with the ⅓ cup stock over heat and add 3 tablespoons of the butter. Bring to a boil, whisking constantly, and keep boiling until the mixture begins to thicken. Now pour the sauce into a food processor, whir 1 minute, and then pour it back into the saucepan. Add the mint, the beans, and the snow peas and reheat over medium heat. Check the seasoning. Put the remaining tablespoon of butter into a non-stick pan. Place the skewers in the pan and cook over high heat until the butter just melts; 1 minute on each side should be enough.

PRESENTATION:

Divide the sauce and vegetables among four warm plates and put one skewer in the middle of each plate.

Matelote de
filets de sole aux poireaux

RED-WINE FISH STEW WITH
SOLE AND LEEKS

TO SERVE 4:

1 pound (about 4) leeks
1 small shallot
7 tablespoons butter, plus extra for the baking dish
½ cup water
Salt and pepper
¾ cup **fish stock** (page 229)
1¼ cups light red wine such as Fleurie, Brouilly, or Beaujolais-
    Village
1 teaspoon sugar
8 lobsterettes (see **NOTES**)
8 Dover sole fillets, about 1 pound in all, or other firm white-
    fleshed fish

PREPARATIONS:

Cut off and discard the dark green leaves from the leeks. Wash the leeks and cut the remaining light-green and white sections into ½-inch dice. Chop the shallot.

Heat 2 tablespoons of the butter in a saucepan, add the leeks, and cook them over moderate heat, stirring, until they begin to soften, about 2 minutes. Then add the water and continue cooking until the liquid completely evaporates, about 5 minutes. Season with salt and pepper, add 1 tablespoon of the butter, and set aside. Brown the shallot in a small heavy saucepan with 1 tablespoon of the butter. Add ½ cup of the fish stock and all the red wine and sugar. Let cook over high heat until the liquid reduces by three quarters to a scant ½ cup. Set it aside.

Shell and devein the tails of the lobsterettes. Butter a metal platter or a baking dish and arrange the sole fillets on it. Salt and pepper them and moisten them with the remaining ¼ cup of fish stock.

Heat the oven to 525°F. Just before putting the sole into the oven, reheat the leeks and the red-wine reduction. Cook the sole fillets in the preheated oven for 3 minutes; add the lobsterettes after 1 minute so that they will cook for 2 minutes. Remove the platter from the oven and pour the cooking juices from the fish into the saucepan with the red-wine reduction. Over medium heat, whisk in the remaining 3 tablespoons of butter. Check the seasoning.

PRESENTATION:

Serve on warm plates with the sole fillets and the lobsterettes arranged on a bed of leeks and nap with the sauce.

NOTES: *You can substitute the meat from 2 raw lobster tails, weighing 8 ounces each in the shell, shelled and cut into ½-inch slices for the lobsterettes. See page 31 for more information on lobsterettes.*
This is also a delicious method for cooking salmon, with no shellfish at all. Ed.

Paupiettes de
sole et saumon au safran

SOLE AND SALMON ROLLS WITH SAFFRON

TO SERVE 4:

1 shallot
2 garlic cloves
4 sprigs chervil (decoration)
3 tomatoes
About ¼ pound little peas in their shells, to yield 2 tablespoons
    shelled, optional
Two ¾-inch-thick salmon steaks, about ¼ pound each
4 large Dover sole fillets, about ¾ pound in all, or other firm
    fine-grained white-fleshed fish

Salt and pepper
4 tablespoons butter
⅔ cup white wine
¼ teaspoon powdered saffron
¼ teaspoon saffron threads
⅓ cup heavy cream

PREPARATIONS:

Chop the shallot and garlic. Pluck the leaves from the chervil sprigs. Peel the tomatoes, seed them, and cut into small dice. If using, shell the peas and cook for 8 minutes in boiling salted water. Drain and set aside.

Remove the skin and bone from the salmon and cut the flesh into ¾-inch cubes. Put the sole fillets, skinned side up, between sheets of waxed paper and pound lightly with a mallet or rolling pin to equalize the thickness. Season. Dot the salmon cubes over the fillets and then roll each fillet up starting with the wider end. Set each fillet roll on end, press lightly on it to flatten it a bit, and then put a toothpick through the roll to hold it together. Butter a small baking dish with 2 tablespoons of the butter, put the rolls in it, and add the garlic and shallots to the dish. Add wine to about one third the height of the rolls.

FINISHING:

Heat the oven to 425°F. Cook the fish in the oven for 6 minutes. Remove the rolls and cut in half crosswise to make pinwheels. Pour the cooking liquid from the dish into a small saucepan. Put the fish back in the baking dish, return the dish to the oven, and turn off the heat. Remove the dish after 1 minute.

Meanwhile, add the saffron powder and threads to the cooking liquid and boil to reduce the liquid by half. Add the cream, tomato dice, and the remaining 2 tablespoons of butter and whisk together. Check the seasoning. If using, add the peas at this point. Continue to boil the sauce for 2 minutes.

PRESENTATION:

Serve two pinwheels per person. Spoon the sauce over the fish and scatter chervil leaves over all.

Filet de féra meunière à la
brunoise de citron, câpres, et tomate

TROUT FILLETS MILLER'S STYLE WITH LIME, CAPERS, AND TOMATO

TO SERVE 4:

2 limes
2 small tomatoes
1 tablespoon capers, drained
1 spring onion (see page 31)
1 small bunch chives
2 teaspoons cream
4 trout fillets, about 3 ounces each (see **NOTE**)
Flour, for dusting the fillets
Salt and pepper
1 tablespoon peanut oil
5 tablespoons butter
1 small bouquet parsley

PREPARATIONS:

With a knife, peel the limes entirely down to the flesh, cut out the sections from between the membranes, and cut the sections into ⅛-inch dice. Peel and seed the tomatoes and cut the flesh into ⅛-inch dice. Chop the capers. Cut the onion into thin slices and chop enough chives to make 1 teaspoon. Brush a little cream on each of the fillets, dip them in flour, and shake to dust off the excess flour. Season them with salt and pepper.

FINISHING:

Heat the oil in a non-stick frying pan over medium-high heat. Sauté the fillets in the oil for 1 minute. Turn them, add 3 tablespoons of the butter to the pan, and continue cooking until the butter foams and the fillets are golden brown.

Remove the fish fillets and put the onions and capers in the oil and butter left in the frying pan. Add the remaining 2 tablespoons of butter and the lime dice and let cook for about 1 minute. Add the tomato dice, check the seasoning, and let cool for 30 seconds longer.

Arrange the four fillets in a fan shape on a hot serving platter, cover them with the sauce, and sprinkle the chopped chives over the sauce. Decorate the platter with the parsley bouquet.

NOTE: *Féra is a delicate, white-fleshed, freshwater fish caught in Lake Geneva and other Swiss lakes. It is similar to the famous omble chevalier (char) of the Lac d'Annecy in France. The best substitutes in the United States are brook trout or lake trout or lake whitefish and in Canada white-fleshed char. Ed.*

Gratin de féra à l'estragon

TROUT GRATIN WITH TARRAGON

TO SERVE 4:

2 branches tarragon
¾ cup heavy cream
2 egg yolks
3 tablespoons butter
Salt and pepper
4 trout fillets, about 3 ounces each (see **NOTE**, preceding
     recipe)
½ cup white wine
¼ lemon

PREPARATIONS:

Chop enough tarragon leaves to make 2 teaspoons. Beat ¼ cup of the cream and mix ⅓ cup of the remaining unwhipped cream with the egg yolks. Butter a flameproof baking dish with 1 tablespoon of the butter. Salt and pepper the trout fillets, arrange them in the dish skin side up, and add the white wine.

FINISHING AND PRESENTATION:

Heat the oven to 450°F. Cook the fillets in the oven for 1½ to 2 minutes, depending on their thickness, just until the skin peels off easily. They should be very underdone since they'll go under the broiler later. Take them out, remove their skins, and arrange the fillets on a heated ovenproof platter. Preheat the broiler.

Add the tarragon to the cooking liquid in the baking dish and reduce by about two thirds over high heat. Now whisk the remaining 2 tablespoons of butter and the final ⅙ cup of the cream into the reduced cooking liquid. Let the mixture reduce over high heat a few moments and then whisk it into the yolk and cream mixture. Pour this sauce into a saucepan and whisk over low heat until it thickens slightly. Remove from the heat and season with salt, pepper, and about 1 teaspoon lemon juice to taste. Finally, carefully fold the whipped cream into the sauce.

Coat the fillets with a thick layer of the sauce and put them under the broiler, close to the heat, just long enough for the sauce to take on a golden color. This should take only about a minute or even less; watch it carefully. Serve immediately and pass the remaining sauce separately.

crustacés et coquillages

CRUSTACEANS & SHELLFISH

NOTE: *The recipes in this chapter are designed as fish courses, almost all to serve four people, before the main course. It is necessary to check the amounts of the principal ingredients first, but you will find that they are usually appropriate to serve two as a main course. Ed.*

Pinces de homard
à la crème de poivrons

LOBSTER CLAWS IN RED PEPPER SAUCE

TO SERVE 4:

16 lobster claws (see **NOTE**)
Salt, pepper, and cayenne
2 tablespoons butter
2 red peppers
2 tablespoons olive oil
⅔ cup heavy cream
¼ cup **vegetable bouillon** (page 228), if needed

PREPARATIONS:

Boil the lobster claws for about 3 minutes. Remove and let cool enough to handle. Crack the claws and remove the meat, trying to keep each claw in one piece. Put the claw meat on a buttered baking dish, season with salt, pepper, and cayenne, and top each claw with a sliver of the butter.

Blanch the red peppers in boiling water for 5 minutes and then peel them. Remove the seeds and the white parts of the peppers and slice the peppers into thin julienne strips. Put the oil in a saucepan over high heat, cook the pepper strips in it for 3 to 4 minutes, and set aside.

FINISHING:

Heat the oven to 400°F. Reheat the pan containing the pepper julienne. Add the cream and reduce over high heat for about 3 minutes. If necessary after reducing, thin the sauce with the vegetable bouillon. Taste and add seasoning if needed. Put the lobster claws in the preheated oven for 2 minutes, just long enough to reheat them.

PRESENTATION:

Serve the claws on heated plates and nap with the pepper sauce.

NOTE: *Rather than 16 lobster claws, you can use the claw and tail meat from four 1-pound lobsters. Cut the meat from each tail in half lengthwise. Ed.*

Cassolette de
homard aux fèves fraîches

LOBSTER WITH FAVA BEANS

TO SERVE 4:

2 pounds fava (or broad) beans in their shells, about ⅔ pound
    or ½ cup shelled (see **NOTES** page 40)
Two 1- to 1¼-pound lobsters
8 tablespoons butter
White portion of 2 leeks
2 garlic cloves
2 spring onions (see page 31)
2 ribs celery
2 tomatoes
⅔ ounce fresh truffles (see page 31)
2 tablespoons olive oil
1 sprig thyme
⅓ cup port
⅓ cup water
⅓ cup heavy cream

PREPARATIONS:

Shell the fava beans and cook them for 2 minutes in salted boiling water. Drain them, let cool slightly so that you can handle them easily, and remove their skins. You will need ½ cup of the cooked beans.

    Cook the lobsters for 1½ minutes in a large pot of salted boiling water. Let cool enough to handle and then remove the meat from the shells. Start by separating the claws from the carcasses. Then remove the tails. Remove the coral and set aside for another dish. Pull apart the body shells or crush with the flat of a cleaver and set aside for making the sauce. Crack the claws, remove the meat in one piece, and set aside in a buttered baking dish. Combine the claw shells with the reserved body shells. Split the tails lengthwise down the middle, remove the pieces of tail meat, take out the intestines, and then put the tail meat in the baking dish with the claw meat. Save the tail shells along with the other shells. Dot the lobster meat with 2 tablespoons of the butter.

    Slice the leeks, cut the garlic cloves in two, dice the onions, and chop the celery. Peel, seed, and chop the tomatoes. Chop the truffles.

Heat the oil in a frying pan over medium heat and add the leeks, garlic, onions, celery, and thyme. Cook for 2 minutes and then add all the lobster shells. Continue to cook for another 3 or 4 minutes, stirring and pressing down on the vegetables to extract their juices. Add the tomatoes and the remaining 6 tablespoons of butter and cook, still over medium heat, for another 2 or 3 minutes. Add the port and the water and reduce slowly over medium heat for 10 minutes. Remove from the heat, strain into a saucepan, and set aside until ready to finish the sauce.

FINISHING:

Heat the oven to 525°F. Put the pan with the sauce over low heat, add the cream, season to taste with salt, pepper, and cayenne, and cook 3 minutes. Pass through a fine strainer and put the sauce back in the pan. Add the beans and the truffles to the sauce and warm over very low heat. Cook the lobster pieces in the preheated oven for 2½ minutes.

PRESENTATION:

Arrange half a lobster tail and one claw on each plate and nap with the sauce.

Langoustines, Saint-Jacques,
et homard aux deux poivres

LOBSTERETTES, SCALLOPS, AND LOBSTER IN PEPPER SAUCE

TO SERVE 4:

Two 1-pound lobsters (see **NOTE**)
4 sea scallops
8 lobsterettes (see **NOTE**)
2 teaspoons black peppercorns
2 teaspoons pink peppercorns
4 shallots
10 tablespoons butter
Salt
2 tablespoons peanut oil

PREPARATIONS:

Boil the lobsters for 2 minutes in salted water. Remove and let cool enough to handle. Twist off the tails and the claws. Cut the tails in half lengthwise and remove the meat. Crack the claws and remove the meat carefully to keep it in one piece. Twist off the lobsterette tails and remove the meat from the tail sections by cutting the ribbed underside with scissors and pulling away the shell so that the meat emerges in one piece.

Crush the black and pink peppercorns together. Chop the shallots and put them in a small frying pan with 6 tablespoons of the butter, the crushed peppercorns, and salt. Cook until the shallots soften and then set aside.

FINISHING:

Heat the oil in a heavy frying pan over high heat. Put in the scallops and let them cook for 1½ minutes. Add the lobsterettes and at the same time turn over the scallops and move them to the edge of the pan so that they will cook more slowly. Half a minute after adding the lobsterettes, put in the pieces of lobster, at the edge of the pan. The lobsterettes should remain in the middle. Half a minute after adding the lobster pieces, turn them and the lobsterettes over and cook 1 minute longer. Add the remaining 4 tablespoons of butter to the pan, let foam, and then baste the shellfish with it. Remove the scallops and the lobsterettes, baste the lobster once more, and then remove. During cooking, adjust the heat, if necessary, so that the shellfish sautés rapidly but the oil doesn't smoke.

Add the cooking oil and butter left in the pan to the shallots and peppercorns and reheat. Check the seasoning and add salt if needed.

PRESENTATION:

Cut the scallops in half horizontally. Arrange the scallops, lobster, and lobsterettes as harmoniously as possible on warm plates. Nap the shellfish with the pepper butter.

NOTE: *See page 31 for information on lobsterettes. The best substitution for this recipe is simply to get 1½-pound instead of 1-pound lobsters, in order to have extra meat to replace that of the lobsterettes. Boil the larger lobsters for 3 minutes rather than 2. Ed.*

Petits choux farcis de
langoustines au beurre de beluga

LOBSTERETTES IN CABBAGE WITH CAVIAR

TO SERVE 4 TO 8:

1 head savoy cabbage
16 large lobsterettes (see **NOTES**)
Salt, pepper, and cayenne
11 tablespoons butter
2 shallots
⅓ cup white wine
1 tablespoon heavy cream
1½ ounces Beluga caviar

PREPARATIONS:

Take 8 nice large leaves from the cabbage and blanch them in a large pot of salted boiling water for 2 to 3 minutes, until they are tender. This might take a bit longer in winter when the leaves are tougher. Drain the blanched leaves and spread out flat on towels.

Twist off the lobsterette tails and remove the meat from the tail sections by cutting the ribbed underside with scissors and pulling away the shell so that the meat emerges in one piece. Season with salt, pepper, and cayenne. Heat 1 tablespoon of the butter in a frying pan over medium heat. Put the lobsterette tails in the pan for about 1 minute, until they just start to firm up and turn white. Remove and set aside.

Remove the large central rib from each drained cabbage leaf. Place each leaf on a work surface and overlap the two sides where the rib was removed to make a continuous surface. Put 2 lobsterette tails, one crossed over the other, on each cabbage leaf. Fold the cabbage leaf around the lobsterettes to make a little packet. Put the packets, folded side down, in a baking dish of a size to hold them all close together. Put ½ tablespoon of butter on each packet and refrigerate. Mince the shallots.

FINISHING:

Heat the oven to 450°F. Put the minced shallots in a small heavy saucepan with the white wine and reduce over medium heat until you have about 2 tablespoons of liquid. While the wine is reducing, cook the cabbage packets in the preheated oven until warm, about 5 minutes. When the white wine is reduced, add the cream to it, bring to a boil, and reduce the heat to very low. Then thicken the sauce by whisking in the remaining 6 tablespoon of butter. Season with salt, pepper, and cayenne.

PRESENTATION:

Put the cabbage packets on warm plates. Pour the cooking butter from the baking dish into the sauce, whisk it in quickly, and surround each packet with sauce. Top each cabbage packet with a teaspoon of caviar. Serve immediately

NOTES: *Serve one or two packets per person depending on the rest of your menu. See page 31 for information on lobsterettes.*
This is a good recipe for lobster. Use the meat of 4 raw lobster tails, weighing 8 ounces each in the shell, cut crosswise into ½-inch slices. Ed.

Grillade de Saint-Jacques et langoustines aux asperges

GRILLED SCALLOPS AND LOBSTERETTES WITH ASPARAGUS

TO SERVE 4:

12 asparagus spears
8 lobsterettes (see **NOTES**)
2 lemons
2 sprigs mint
Salt and pepper
2 tablespoons olive oil
8 sea scallops (see **NOTES**)

PREPARATIONS:

Cut off the ends of the asparagus so that the spears are about 4 inches long. Peel the spears carefully. Cook the asparagus in salted boiling water until tender, 5 to 10 minutes. Drain on paper towels.

Twist off the lobsterette tails and remove the meat from the tail sections by cutting the ribbed underside with scissors and pulling away the shell so that the meat emerges in one piece. Squeeze the lemons and measure out 4 tablespoons juice. Chop enough mint to make 1 tablespoon.

FINISHING:

Put the lemon juice in a small saucepan, add salt and pepper, and whisk in the olive oil. Put the dressing over low heat and heat it to lukewarm. Add the mint and remove from the heat. Reheat the asparagus spears, if necessary, by putting them in a colander and dipping them into a pan of boiling water. Remove and let drain while you grill the scallops and lobsterettes.

Season the lobsterettes and scallops with salt and pepper and grill them, 2 minutes for the scallops and 1 minute for the lobsterettes. If you don't have a grill, cook them in a non-stick frying pan, over high heat, with a few drops of olive oil. Use the same cooking times.

PRESENTATION:

Serve on warm plates with three spears of asparagus arranged in a fan shape at the top of each plate, two scallops in the middle, and two crisscrossed lobsterettes below them. Pour the lemon and mint dressing over all.

NOTES: *Two raw lobster tails, weighing 6 to 8 ounces in the shell, shelled and cut crosswise into ½-inch slices can be substituted for the lobsterettes. See page 31 for information on lobsterettes.*

The asparagus and dressing are good accompaniments just for scallops. Double the quantity of scallops. Ed.

SCALLOP AND LOBSTERETTE PAPILLOTES WITH CORIANDER

TO SERVE 4:

8 sea scallops, with coral (see **NOTES**)
4 large or 8 small lobsterettes (see **NOTES**)
1 teaspoon pink peppercorns
½ teaspoon coriander seeds
Salt and pepper
2 spring onions (see page 31)
5 blades chives
10 tablespoons butter
1 tomato
⅓ cup white wine

PREPARATIONS:

Cut the scallops in half horizontally and keep only 4 of the corals, one per person. Twist off the lobsterette tails and remove the meat from the tail sections by cutting the ribbed underside with scissors and pulling away the shell so that the meat emerges in one piece. Crush the peppercorns and coriander seeds in a mortar with a pestle or grind in a pepper mill. Season the scallops, coral, and lobsterettes with salt, pepper, and half the crushed spices.

Cut the onions into thin slices and chop enough chives to make 1 teaspoon. Heat 4 tablespoons of the butter in a non-stick frying pan over medium heat. Add the sliced onions and half the chives. Put the scallops in the pan and cook them 20 seconds per side. Remove to a plate and add the lobsterettes, which should cook until firm, but no more, about 30 seconds per side. Remove them to the plate and finally cook the coral for 2 minutes in all, turning several times. Set aside the frying pan and its contents, which you will use later.

From sulfurized paper, cut 4 ovals 15 inches long and 8 inches wide. Mark the middle by making a lengthwise crease and butter each paper lightly. Arrange 4 scallop halves, 1 coral, and 1 lobsterette tail in a row just below each crease. Pour over them the butter and onions from the frying pan. Fold over the top half of each paper oval and make a rolled border about ⅓ inch wide around each curve, pleating as you fold the edges to seal well.

Peel and seed the tomato and cut it into ¼-inch dice.

FINISHING:

Heat the oven to 525°F. Cook the papillotes on a baking sheet in the oven for 3½ minutes. At the same time, put the wine in a small heavy saucepan, bring to a boil over medium heat, and let it boil for 30 seconds. Reduce heat to very low and thicken the sauce lightly by whisking in the remaining 6 tablespoons of butter. The sauce need not be too thick; you are not making a beurre blanc. Season the sauce to taste with salt and the rest of the crushed spices. Add the tomato and the remaining chives.

PRESENTATION:

Put the papillotes on plates and use scissors to cut out semicircular lids about 1 inch from the edges. Pour the sauce into the papillotes.

NOTES: *Get scallops with coral if possible. If not, simply omit the coral and make the rest of the recipe as described.*

One raw lobster tail, weighing 8 ounces in the shell, shelled and cut crosswise into ½-inch slices can be substituted for the lobsterettes. See page 31 for information on lobsterettes. Ed.

Saint-Jacques aux endives et au citron vert

SCALLOPS WITH ENDIVES AND LIME

TO SERVE 4:

1 pound Belgian endives
8 sea scallops, with coral (see **NOTE**)
1 lime
½ lemon
1 tablespoon sugar
Salt, pepper, and cayenne
8 tablespoons butter
A few drops oil
3 tablespoons white wine
3 tablespoons port
1½ teaspooons heavy cream

PREPARATIONS:

Cut each endive on the diagonal, giving it a quarter turn after each cut so that you get triangular pieces. Separate the leaves and put them in a bowl. Separate the coral from the scallop meat.

Cut a ½-inch-wide strip of zest from the lime and then cut it into long, very thin julienne strips. Squeeze 2 tablespoons juice from the lime. Into a separate bowl, squeeze 1 tablespoon lemon juice.

FINISHING:

Season the endives with the lime juice, the sugar, salt, and a few turns of a pepper mill. Mix together carefully with your hands. Melt 2 tablespoons of the butter in a large saucepan over high heat, add the endives, and cook 2 minutes. Add 2 teaspoons of the lemon juice and continue cooking over high heat, stirring, for 1 minute. Remove from heat.

Season the scallops with salt, pepper, and cayenne. Heat the oil over high heat in a non-stick pan. When it is quite hot, sauté the scallops and their coral exactly 1 minute on each side. Remove and set aside. Pour the white wine and port into a small heavy saucepan and reduce by half over high heat. Add the cream, bring to a boil twice, stirring each time to interrupt the boiling, and then lower the heat and thicken the sauce by whisking in the remaining 6 tablespoons of butter in pieces. Season with salt, pepper, and the remaining 1 teaspoon lemon juice.

PRESENTATION:

Arrange a quarter of the endives on the lower part of each of four small heated plates. Put two scallops and two coral above the endives, nap the scallops with the sauce, and garnish them with the lime zest.

NOTE: *Get scallops with coral if possible. If not, simply omit the coral and either make the rest of the recipe exactly as described or include an extra scallop per person. Ed.*

Saint-Jacques en feuilleté aux deux purées

SCALLOPS IN PUFF PASTRY
WITH TWO PURÉES

TO SERVE 4:

½ pound **puff pastry** (page 241)
1 to 1½ pounds little peas in their shells, about 1 cup shelled
Salt, pepper, and cayenne
1 pinch sugar
½ cup heavy cream
2 shallots
1 sprig each, chervil, parsley, and tarragon
1 blade chive
8 sea scallops, with coral (see **NOTES**)
5 tablespoons butter
¼ lemon

PREPARATIONS:

Heat the oven to 425°F. Roll out the puff pastry and cut it into 4 rectangles each about 3½ inches by 2½ inches. Turn them over and put them on a baking sheet. (Refrigerate if not baking immediately.) Bake the puff pastry in the preheated oven for 10 minutes. Reduce the oven temperature to 375°F and continue baking until thoroughly cooked, 15 to 20 minutes.

Shell the peas and cook them in a large pan of salted boiling water until tender, about 10 minutes (5 minutes if frozen). Drain them and purée in a food processor or push them through a fine sieve. Season with salt, pepper, and a pinch of sugar. Add ¼ cup of the cream and cook the purée over low heat until it is fairly thick. Check the seasoning and set the pea purée aside until ready to serve.

Mince the shallots. Chop all the herbs together to make 1 tablespoon in all. Separate the coral from the scallop meat and cut the scallops into ½-inch dice.

Sauté the scallop coral over medium heat in 1 tablespoon of the butter for 2 minutes, add half the chopped shallots, and continue cooking another minute. Remove from the heat and whir the coral in the food processor to purée. Put the puréed coral in a saucepan with 2 tablespoons of the butter, the remaining ¼ cup cream, and salt and pepper. Reduce the purée over low heat for 2 minutes until it thickens and then check the seasoning and add lemon juice to taste, about 1 teaspoon. Set aside until ready to serve.

Heat the oven to 350°F. Slice the puff pastries in two horizontally, cutting about one third of the way down from the top. Put the pastries in the preheated oven to reheat. Reheat the two purées over low heat.

Season the scallop dice with salt, pepper, and cayenne. Heat a frying pan over high heat. Add the remaining 2 tablespoons of butter and when it foams put in the scallop dice, the remaining shallots, and the mixed herbs. Sauté the scallops so quickly that they only heat through; about 30 seconds is long enough.

PRESENTATION:

Spread a quarter of the pea purée on the bottom half of each piece of heated puff pastry. Divide the scallops over the layer of pea purée and cover the scallops with the coral purée. Cover with the puff pastry tops and serve immediately, as is or with a light anchovy butter.

NOTES: *If scallops with coral are unavailable, use anchovy butter in place of coral purée.*

Two-thirds pound of bay scallops can be used instead of the sea-scallop dice.

For anchovy butter, mix together 3 tablespoons softened sweet butter, ½ teaspoon lemon juice, and 1 teaspoon anchovy paste. Use at room temperature. Ed.

Mousse de Saint-Jacques à la citronnette

SCALLOP MOUSSE WITH LEMON SAUCE

TO SERVE 6 TO 12:

⅔ pound sea scallops, with coral (see **NOTE**)
Salt, pepper, and cayenne
1 whole egg
1 tablespoon cognac
1 tablespoon port
1½ cups heavy cream
2 ounces (4 tablespoons) caviar
1 lemon
6 tablespoons olive oil
2 sprigs dill
1 tomato

PREPARATIONS:

Separate the coral from the scallop meat. You'll use 6 coral for this recipe. Simmer the coral in a saucepan with about ⅓ inch of water for 5 minutes. Drain the cooked coral and then cut them into ¼-inch cubes.

Put the scallops and a pinch of salt in the food processor and whir until puréed. Add the egg and whir until it is blended in. Season with a good pinch of cayenne and an equal amount of pepper and then add the cognac and port. Whir in the cream, adding it slowly in a thin stream. Check the seasoning; it should be quite spicy with a definite flavor of cayenne and pepper. Transfer to a bowl and fold the coral cubes into the mousse mixture.

Butter 12 small soufflé molds about 2 inches in diameter. Fill the molds halfway with the mousse mixture and then put 1 teaspoon of caviar in the middle of each mold. Fill the molds with the rest of the mousse and then tap them on the table to level them.

Squeeze the lemon and put 3 tablespoons of the juice into a small saucepan with the olive oil and salt and pepper. Chop enough dill to make 1 tablespoon. Peel and seed the tomato and cut it into tiny dice. Add the dill and diced tomato to the lemon and olive oil mixture.

FINISHING:

Heat the oven to 425°F. Put the soufflé molds in a baking dish and add warm water to the dish to come halfway up the molds. Lay a buttered sheet of sulfurized paper or aluminum foil over the molds and cook them in the preheated oven for 10 to 15 minutes until just barely set. Warm the lemon sauce over low heat until lukewarm.

PRESENTATION:

Serve one or two mousses to each person depending on the menu. Set a warm plate on top of each mold in turn (two at a time if you're serving two per person) and flip over to unmold and then surround with the lemon sauce.

NOTE: *Although scallop coral adds color, flavor, and texture to the mousse, it is not absolutely necessary. If you can't get coral, simply omit it. Ed.*

OYSTERS GIRARDET

TO SERVE 4:

1 carrot
White part of 1 leek
1 rib celery
16 oysters
½ cup champagne
1 tablespoon heavy cream
6 tablespoons butter
Salt, pepper, and cayenne

PREPARATIONS:

Slice all the vegetables into julienne strips about 2½ to 3 inches long. Open the oysters, remove them from the shells, and filter their liquor through a cheesecloth-lined strainer into a small heavy pan. If you buy the oysters already opened, be sure to ask for their liquor. Add the champagne to the pan and reduce over high heat until you have about ¼ cup liquid.

FINISHING:

Bring a saucepan of salted water to a boil. Reheat the champagne reduction, add the cream, bring to a boil, and then thicken the sauce by whisking in the butter in pieces. Season with salt, pepper, and cayenne. Cook the julienned vegetables in the boiling water until just tender, about 1 minute, and drain. Put the oysters into the butter and champagne sauce and leave them over low heat for 30 seconds, just long enough to heat them.

PRESENTATION:

Put the oysters on heated plates, sprinkle the vegetables around them, and nap with the sauce. Serve immediately.

Huîtres chaudes aux courgettes

WARM OYSTERS WITH ZUCCHINI

TO SERVE 4:

12 oysters
Seaweed for presentation (see **COMMENT**)
3 zucchini
½ lemon
½ cup heavy cream
½ pound (2 sticks) butter
Salt, pepper, and cayenne

PREPARATIONS:

Open the oysters, pour their liquor through a cheesecloth-lined strainer into a small heavy saucepan, and reduce over high heat to ¼ cup. Set the oysters aside until ready to finish the dish. Arrange a bed of seaweed on each of 4 large plates and put the deep halves of the oyster shells on the seaweed. Slice the zucchini into very thin rounds (you'll need about 10 slices per oyster). Blanch the zucchini slices in salted boiling water for 2 minutes and then drain. Squeeze 4 teaspoons lemon juice.

FINISHING AND PRESENTATION:

Bring the reduced oyster liquor to a boil and add the cream. Let it reduce over high heat for 1 minute. Finish the sauce by whisking in 12 tablespoons of the butter, bit by bit, still at a boil. When all the butter is absorbed, add the lemon juice and then remove the pan from the heat and check the seasoning. Whisk the sauce another minute or so off the heat. (*NOTE: It is essential to whisk at this point to bring the temperature down, or the sauce will separate. An easier method is to thicken the sauce with the butter over very low heat. Ed.*)

Melt the remaining 4 tablespoons of butter over medium heat in a non-stick frying pan and add the zucchini. Season with salt, pepper, and cayenne, cook just long enough to warm, and then remove from the heat. Put the oysters in the sauce and put the pan over very low heat for about 30 seconds. Shake the pan gently with a circular motion while heating the oysters. Remove the oysters from the sauce and place them in the shells on the bed of seaweed. Quickly arrange the zucchini rounds on top of each oyster, overlapping them. Whisk the sauce again for a few seconds over very low heat and then lightly coat each zucchini-topped oyster with it. Serve immediately.

COMMENT: A simpler presentation, less aesthetically successful than the one described above, is to serve the oysters in cassolettes (individual pans) or in small soup plates.

volailles

POULTRY

Aile de volaille
aux poireaux et aux truffes

CHICKEN BREASTS WITH LEEKS AND TRUFFLES

TO SERVE 4:

4 chicken breasts, with the wings atttached
4 large leeks
2 shallots
3 ounces fresh truffles (see **NOTES**)
Salt and pepper
2 cups **chicken stock** (page 232)
3 tablespoons truffle juice (see **NOTES**)
10 tablespoons butter
⅔ cup water
⅓ cup heavy cream

PREPARATIONS:

Cut off the wing tip and first joint, leaving the little drumstick-shaped piece of wing on the breast. Bone the breasts but leave the remaining wing joint attached. Make a horizontal slit in each of the suprêmes, cutting between the two muscles to form a pocket for the truffle stuffing.

Cut off and discard the dark green leaves from the leeks. Wash the white and light-green sections. Slice them in quarters lengthwise and then crosswise into ½-inch pieces and separate the layers. Chop the shallots. Slice half the truffles and cut the other half into large dice.

Stuff the chicken breasts with the truffle slices. Salt and pepper the inside of the cavities and then close with toothpicks. Put ¾ cup of the chicken stock in a pan with 2 tablespoons of the truffle juice. Reduce over high heat until there are only about 4 tablespoons of liquid left. Set aside.

FINISHING:

Bring the remaining 1 ¼ cups chicken stock to a simmer in a pan large enough to hold the chicken breasts. Salt and pepper the breasts and then simmer them over low heat, uncovered, for 8 to 10 minutes. The flesh should remain moist and still be pink in the center.

While the chicken is cooking, melt 4 tablespoons of the butter in a frying pan over high heat and add the shallots and the leeks. Stir for 1 minute and then add the water and cook until the water completely evaporates, 3 to 4 minutes. Now add the cream and the diced truffle and cook over high heat until the cream thickens and coats the vegetables. The leeks should still be a bit crisp. Finish the leek mixture by whisking in 2 tablespoons of the butter and the remaining tablespoon of the truffle juice. Season.

Now reheat the chicken-stock and truffle-juice reduction and thicken it by whisking in the remaining 4 tablespoons of butter. Check the seasoning.

PRESENTATION:

Arrange the leeks and truffles on warm plates. Lift the chicken breasts out of their stock, remove the picks, and put the breasts on top of the leeks. Nap with the sauce.

NOTES: *A less expensive version of this dish can be made using about ⅓ cup dry wild mushrooms, reconstituted in warm water, to stuff the chicken breasts and a few diced fresh mushrooms rather than truffles in the leek garnish. In this case, use the dry mushroom soaking liquid in place of the truffle juice.*

Of course, the truffles make the better dish. For information on truffles and truffle juice see page 31. Ed.

Poularde pochée à la crème de cresson

POACHED CHICKEN WITH WATERCRESS SAUCE

TO SERVE 4:

¾ pound watercress
6 tablespoons butter, softened
¼ lemon
8 new radishes or small white turnips
9 small carrots
12 small new potatoes
4 medium leeks
2 small celery roots
One 3-pound chicken
2 quarts **chicken stock** (page 232)
1 onion
Salt
½ cup heavy cream

PREPARATIONS:

Cut or twist the large stems off the watercress and whir the leaves in the food processor until they are liquid. With the processor still running, add the butter to the liquid, a bit at a time. Refrigerate this watercress butter.

Squeeze the lemon quarter. Peel the radishes, carrots, and potatoes. Cut off and discard the leek greens and cut each white part crosswise to make two pieces. Peel the celery roots, cut into quarters, and trim the sections into the shape of large garlic cloves. Coat them with the lemon juice. Truss the chicken.

COOKING:

Put the chicken stock in a pot that will just hold the chicken. Add 1 of the carrots, 1 of the leeks, and the onion to the stock, salt moderately, and bring to a boil. Put the chicken in the pot, reduce the heat, and poach for 30 minutes with the liquid at a bare simmer. Turn the chicken over halfway through the cooking time.

While the chicken is poaching, prepare the vgetables by cooking them in salted boiling water. Cook the radishes and celery root together, the remaining 8 carrots, 3 leeks, and the potatoes each in separate pans. Cooking times are difficult to state because they vary with the size and freshness of the vegetables. They should all be cooked until almost done and then removed from the heat and left to stand in their respective cooking liquids to finish cooking and to keep warm until the chicken is ready. (**NOTE:** *If you don't have enough burners for so many pots, cook the carrots or the leeks ahead and reheat briefly in boiling water or the chicken cooking liquid just before serving. Ed.)*

When the chicken is done, take it from the pot, remove the trussing strings, and let it wait while you finish the sauce. Take 1 cup of the cooking liquid from the chicken and reduce over high heat to $\frac{1}{3}$ cup. Remove from the heat, add the cream, and then bring back to a full boil. Finish the sauce by whisking in the watercress butter, little by little, over high heat.

PRESENTATION:

Carve the chicken and serve it like a pot-au-feu, with the chicken surrounded by the vegetables in shallow bowls and the sauce on the side in a sauceboat. And why not serve the bouillon along with it in cups?

COMMENT: It's an interesting decorative touch to put a few nice watercress leaves between the skin and the flesh of the chicken along each breast. Do this before trussing the bird.

Poularde de Bresse braisée
aux endives et au poivre vert

BRAISED CHICKEN WITH ENDIVES AND GREEN PEPPERCORNS

TO SERVE 4:

One 3-pound chicken
Salt and pepper
1 carrot
½ rib celery
1 shallot
2 pounds Belgian endives
2 lemons
2 tablespoons peanut oil
13 tablespoons butter
¼ onion
2 garlic cloves
⅓ cup port
⅓ cup **chicken stock** (page 232)
1 tablespoon sugar
4 teaspoons green peppercorns, drained

PREPARATIONS:

Salt and pepper the chicken inside and out and truss it. Chop the carrot and the celery and cut the shallot in half. Cut the endives in triangular pieces by cutting diagonally, giving the endive a quarter turn, and cutting again. Continue rotating and cutting until the endives are all sliced. Separate the leaves and put them in a bowl. Squeeze ¼ cup lemon juice.

COOKING:

Heat the oven to 400°F. Heat the oil in a roasting pan over high heat and when it's very hot put in the chicken. Brown it on all sides. This should take around 10 minutes.

When the chicken is golden all over, remove it and pour the oil out of the pan. Replace it with 4 tablespoons of the butter and let it melt. Put the chicken back in the pan on its side and add the carrot, celery, shallot, onion, and garlic. Roast the chicken in the preheated oven for 20 minutes, basting often with the pan juices and turning it carefully from one side to the other and finally onto its back so that it cooks on all sides. Be careful also to watch the oven so that it does not overheat and burn the butter or the vegetables. When the chicken is done, remove from the roasting pan and discard the fat but leave the vegetables in the pan.

Start to prepare the sauce by holding the chicken over the roasting pan and draining the juices from the inside of the bird into the pan. Add 2 tablespoons of the butter to the roasting pan. Put the pan over medium heat and pour in the port. Let it boil while scraping the bottom of the pan firmly with a wooden spatula to get all the coagulated juices into the sauce. Add the chicken stock, bring the sauce back to a boil, and then strain it into a saucepan. Press the vegetables to get all their juices and discard the vegetables. Set the sauce aside for a few minutes while you prepare the endives.

Season the endives with the sugar, 3 pinches of salt, 10 turns of the pepper mill, and 3 tablespoons of the lemon juice. Mix well. Heat 1 ½ tablespoons of the butter in each of two frying pans and add half the endive to each. Cook over high heat for 3 minutes, stirring two or three times. Remove to a heated serving plate.

Bring the sauce to a boil. Add the green peppercorns and the remaining tablespoon of lemon juice and then thicken the sauce by whisking in the remaining 4 tablespoons of butter.

PRESENTATION:

Put the chicken, either whole or cut into quarters, on top of the endives on a heated serving platter. Coat the chicken very lightly with sauce and serve the rest of the sauce in a sauceboat.

Fricassée de volaille
aux concombres et à la tomate

CHICKEN FRICASSEE WITH CUCUMBERS AND TOMATO

TO SERVE 4:

½ carrot
½ onion
½ of the white part of a leek
¼ rib celery
1 garlic clove
One 3-pound chicken
2 small cucumbers
1 sprig parsley
5 blades chives
1 tomato
1 tablespoon peanut oil
1 sprig thyme
Salt and pepper
6 tablespoons butter
⅔ cup white wine
3 tablespoons port
3 tablespoons madeira
⅔ cup heavy cream

PREPARATIONS:

Chop the carrot, onion, leek, celery, and garlic. Cut the chicken so that you have 6 pieces—2 legs, 2 thighs, and 2 breasts. Cut the backbone and the ribs into pieces to use later and put the wings aside for use in a different dish. Peel the cucumbers, quarter lengthwise, remove the seeds, and cut each quarter into 1½-inch pieces. Trim each cucumber piece into the shape of a garlic clove. Chop the parsley and the chives. Peel the tomato, seed it, and cut the flesh into small dice.

COOKING:

Heat the oven to 525°F. In a heavy flameproof casserole large enough to hold the chicken pieces as well as the bones, heat the oil over medium-high heat. Add the carrot, onion, leek, celery, garlic, thyme, and the pieces of the chicken carcass. Cook for 3 minutes, stirring, to brown the vegetables and bones.

Season the chicken pieces with salt and pepper and arrange them in the casserole, skin side up. Dot them with 4 tablespoons of the butter and then cook over medium heat for 5 minutes. Turn the chicken pieces over and slide the casserole into the preheated oven. Remove the white meat pieces after 5 minutes and keep them warm on a serving platter. After 5 more minutes, remove the casserole from the oven, remove the remaining pieces of chicken, and add to the platter. While the chicken is cooking, blanch the cucumbers in salted boiling water for 3 to 5 minutes. When they are translucent, they are done. Remove and drain.

Pour the wine, port, and madeira into the casserole with the vegetables and bones. Bring to a boil and scrape the bottom of the pan carefully to incorporate the cooked-on juices. Cook over medium-high heat for 3 minutes and then strain the juices into a small saucepan. Bring to boil twice, stirring each time to interrupt the boiling, and then add the cream and continue to boil rapidly until the sauce thickens lightly. This will take about 2 minutes. Now add the cucumbers and continue cooking the sauce until it just naps the back of a spoon, another 1 or 2 minutes. Finish the sauce by whisking in the remaining 2 tablespoons of butter. Check for seasoning and add the tomato dice.

PRESENTATION:

Arrange the tomato dice and pieces of cucumber around the chicken pieces on a serving platter and coat the chicken with the remaining sauce. Sprinkle with the parsley and chives.

ROAST DUCK WITH SALSIFY

TO SERVE 2:

One 3½-pound duck (see **NOTES**)
Salt and pepper
4 salsify roots, about 6 ounces in all (see **NOTES**)
1 small shallot
2 garlic cloves
1 sprig flat-leaf parsley
2 tablespoons peanut oil
5 tablespoons butter
3 tablespoons red-wine vinegar
3 tablespoons port

PREPARATIONS:

Cut the wings off the duck at the second joint. Reserve the heart and the liver. Remove any excess fat from the inside of the duck and season it inside and out. Truss the duck.

Peel the salsify and cut them into small sticks about 1 inch long and ¼ inch wide. Mince the shallot and cut the garlic into very, very thin slices. Chop enough parsley to make 1 teaspoon. Chop the duck liver and heart into small bits.

COOKING:

Heat the oven to 450°F. Heat 1 tablespoon of the oil in a roasting pan over high heat. When the oil is quite hot, place the duck on its side in the pan and sear for 2 minutes. Then turn it on the other side for 2 minutes.

Leave the duck on its side and put it in the preheated oven. Cook it for 20 minutes in all, 8 minutes on one side, 8 minutes on the other side, and then for the last 4 minutes on its back. Remove the duck from the oven, untruss it, and pour the juices in the cavity into the sauce you will have started while the duck was cooking. Put the duck on a heated platter and let it rest in a warm place for 10 minutes before serving.

While the duck is roasting, cook the salsify. Heat the remaining tablespoon of oil in a small frying pan over medium-high heat, add the salsify, and cook, stirring constantly, for 2 minutes. Lower the heat to medium and continue cooking for 5 minutes, turning the salsify occasionally. Reduce the heat if the salsify threatens to burn. Season with salt and pepper and add 1 tablespoon of the butter. Continue cooking over low heat until tender, 5 to 8 minutes more. Set aside to wait until ready to serve the duck.

Start to prepare the sauce by melting 1 tablespoon of the butter in a small saucepan. Add the garlic and shallot and sauté gently for 3 minutes to brown. Add the vinegar and port and cook over medium heat another minute. Remove from the heat.

When you take the duck out of the oven, pour the juices from the cavity into the sauce. Reheat the sauce, season with salt and pepper, and whisk in 2 tablespoons of the butter to thicken it lightly. Add a few drops of vinegar and the parsley. Reheat the salsify. Just before serving the duck, sauté the chopped duck liver and heart in the remaining 1 tablespoon of butter over high heat for 30 seconds.

PRESENTATION:

Present the duck whole, surrounded by the salsify. Pour a little bit of the sauce over the duck and sprinkle it with the chopped liver and heart. Serve the rest of the sauce in a sauceboat.

NOTES: *European ducks are meatier and less fatty than our readily available Long Island variety. A Muscovy duck works well in this recipe.*

Salsify, also called oyster root or oyster plant, is available in late fall and early winter. Ed.

DUCK WITH SPRING VEGETABLES

TO SERVE 2:

2 turnips, about ½ pound in all
6 spring onions, with stems (see page 31)
2 ounces snow peas, about ½ cup
2 ounces green beans, about ½ cup
¾ pound little peas in their shells, about ½ cup shelled
4 tablespoons butter
One 3½-pound duck (see **NOTES,** preceding recipe)
Salt and pepper
1½ tablespoons peanut oil
¼ cup sugar
2 tablespoons sherry vinegar
¼ cup **white stock** (page 233)
¾ cup **veal stock** (page 234)
A few drops white wine, if needed to thin the sauce

PREPARATIONS:

Peel the turnips and then cut each into 12 wedges. Cut off the stems of the spring onions so they are no longer than 2 inches. Peel the onions down to the first layer of tender skin. String the snow peas and beans and cut them into ½-inch pieces. Shell the little peas.

Bring a pan of salted water to a boil and put the beans in it. After 2 minutes, add the small peas and then the snow peas 30 seconds later. Let cook 2 minutes longer and check to see whether the vegetables are tender. Remove the vegetables with a skimmer or slotted spoon, put them in a saucepan with ½ tablespoon of the butter, and set aside. Blanch the onions in the same water for 5 minutes, drain, put them in a pan with ½ tablespoon of the butter, and set them aside also.

Cut off the wings of the duck at the second joints and remove any fat from the duck cavity. Season the duck inside and out and truss it.

Brown the turnips in a frying pan with ½ tablespoon of the oil. Stir them so they brown uniformly. Set the turnips aside for a few minutes while you start the sauce. Put the sugar in a saucepan over low heat and let it melt and then cook until it turns a caramel color. Pour in the vinegar, white stock, and ¼ cup of the veal stock. Mix together carefully and let cook 3 or 4 minutes until the caramel dissolves. Put the browned turnip pieces into this sauce and boil for 3 minutes. Remove the pan from the heat, take the turnips out of the sauce with a slotted spoon, and reserve. Set the sauce aside.

COOKING:

Heat the oven to 475°F. Heat the remaining tablespoon of oil in a roasting pan over high heat. Put the duck in the pan on its side and let it sear for 2 minutes. Then turn it on the other side to sear for another 2 minutes.

Put the duck, still on its side, in the preheated oven. Let it roast for 8 minutes, then turn it to the other side to roast 8 minutes, and finally turn it on its back for 4 minutes. Take it from the oven, remove the trussing strings, put it on a heated platter, and leave in a warm place for 10 minutes to rest.

Pour off the fat from the roasting pan, put in the remaining ½ cup veal stock, and bring to a boil over high heat. Scrape the bottom of the pan to deglaze the duck juices. Add 3 tablespoons of the butter and the caramel sauce. Mix well and then put the duck back in the roaster. Glaze it by basting it continuously for 2 minutes over medium-high heat. Remove the duck from the roasting pan and drain the juices from the cavity into the roasting pan. Put the duck on a long serving platter.

Reheat the green vegetables and the onions and season to taste. Taste the sauce and correct seasoning. If the sauce is too thick, thin it with a few drops of white wine. Bring it to a final boil and put the turnip pieces back into the sauce to reheat.

PRESENTATION:

Present the duck in the center of the platter with the pieces of turnip around it and the sauce in a sauceboat. Put three of the onions at each end of the platter and arrange the green vegetables along the sides. Carve and serve immediately.

GUINEA HEN WITH NEW TURNIPS

TO SERVE 2:

16 very small white turnips with greens, about 1 pound in all
Salt and pepper
4½ tablespoons butter, plus extra for the baking dish
½ carrot
¼ rib celery
1 sprig parsley
One 1-pound guinea hen
1 teaspoon peanut oil
8 garlic cloves
⅓ cup **vegetable bouillon** (page 228), optional

PREPARATIONS:

Cut off the ends of the turnip greens leaving 2½ inches attached to the root. Peel the turnips neatly, cutting off the skin in vertical strips. Protect the greens of each turnip by wrapping them in a small piece of aluminum foil. Cook the turnips in salted boiling water until they can be easily pierced with a pointed knife, 7 to 10 minutes. The fresher the turnips, the less cooking time is needed. Drain and let cool.

Remove the aluminum foil from the greens and cut each turnip into quarters. Butter a metal platter or shallow baking dish and arrange the turnip quarters on it. Season them with salt and pepper, distribute 2 tablespoons of the butter over the turnips in small flakes, and set aside.

Chop the carrot and celery and chop a good-size pinch of parsley. Season the hen with salt and pepper, truss it, and rub ½ tablespoon of the butter over the breast.

COOKING:

Heat the oven to 525°F. Put the guinea hen in a small frying pan, resting against the side of the pan so that one side of the breast is against the bottom. Brown over medium heat, add the oil so that the butter on the breast doesn't burn, and brown the other side. When the breast is lightly browned, remove the hen from the pan and place it on its side in a small casserole. Add the garlic cloves, unpeeled, and the carrot and celery. Put 1 tablespoon of the butter on the exposed breast and put the casserole in the preheated oven. Roast for 10 minutes in all, basting often. After 5 minutes, turn the hen on its other side and, 2 minutes before it's done, untruss it and set it on its back to finish cooking the legs. When the hen is done, remove it from the oven and at the same time turn the oven down to 400°F and put the turnips in to reheat for about 5 minutes.

Cut the guinea hen in two and remove the backbone and the ribs. Remove the vegetables and garlic from the casserole with a slotted spoon, throw away the fat, and return the vegetables and garlic to the casserole. Break up the bones removed from the hen and add them to the casserole. Cook a minute over high heat and then add ⅓ cup vegetable bouillon or water and cook for 5 more minutes, scraping the bottom of the casserole and pressing the bones several times to force all their juices into the sauce. Pour the sauce through a strainer into a small pan and press the vegetables through. Season the sauce to taste and reheat it. Thicken by whisking in the remaining 1 tablespoon of butter. Add the parsley.

PRESENTATION:

Serve each half guinea hen on a warm plate with half the turnips arranged in a semicircle at the top of the plate, their green stems toward the edge. Nap the hen with the sauce.

Pigeon au chou

SQUAB WITH CABBAGE

TO SERVE 2:

6 leaves savoy cabbage
2 thin slices bacon
1 onion
3 garlic cloves
1 sprig parsley
Salt and pepper
One 1-pound squab
3½ tablespoons butter
1 teaspoon peanut oil
⅓ cup **white stock** (page 233)

PREPARATIONS:

Remove the large central ribs from 6 large leaves of the savoy cabbage and quarter the leaves. Blanch the cabbage leaves for 1 minute in salted boiling water, refresh them under cold water, and drain. Cut the bacon slices crosswise into thin julienne strips. Chop the onion. Peel the garlic cloves and leave them whole. Chop enough parsley to make ¼ teaspoon. Salt and pepper the squab, put the garlic cloves in the cavity, and truss the bird. Rub ½ tablespoon of the butter over the breast.

COOKING:

Heat the oven to 525°F. Heat the oil in a small frying pan over medium heat. Place the squab breast side down in a small frying pan. Rest it for 1 to 2 minutes on one side of the breast and then on the other until both have lightly browned, holding the pigeon in place if need be.

When the breasts have browned, remove the squab from the pan and place it on its side in a small casserole. Put 1 tablespoon of butter on the exposed breast so that it does not dry out during roasting. Put the squab in the preheated oven for 7 minutes. Baste it often and after 3 minutes turn it on its other side. After that side has also roasted for 3 minutes, turn the squab on its back and remove the trussing string. Make sure you keep basting the squab during its entire 7-minute roasting time.

Remove the squab from the oven, take out the garlic cloves and save them, and discard the cooking fat. Carve the squab by removing the breast meat with the wings attached and then the legs. Keep warm. Break the carcass into several pieces and put it, with the garlic, in a small frying pan. Add the stock and 1 tablespoon water. Cook over high heat for 5 minutes, pressing the bones occasionally so that they release all their juices. After 5 minutes, remove from the heat and discard the carcass pieces. Strain the juices through a fine sieve and force the garlic through the sieve. Set aside in a small pan.

Melt 1½ tablespoons of the butter in a saucepan over low heat with the bacon julienne and the chopped onion. When the butter starts to foam, add the cabbage. Season with salt and pepper and then let simmer 6 to 8 minutes over low heat.

Finish the sauce by bringing the stock and garlic mixture to a boil and then whisking into it the remaining ½ tablespoon of butter. Check the seasoning and, if necessary, thin the sauce with a teaspoon of water. Add the chopped parsley and remove the sauce from the heat.

PRESENTATION:

Mound the cabbage on warm plates and top with the pieces of squab. Coat the squab with the sauce and serve.

POACHED SQUAB WITH VEGETABLES AND FOIE GRAS

TO SERVE 2:

4 small turnips
4 small carrots
2 spring onions, with stems (see page 31)
1 small head savoy cabbage
4 garlic cloves
1 shallot
6 tablespoons butter
¾ cup red wine, plus a few drops for finishing the sauce
3 tablespoons **veal stock** (page 234)
1 quart **white stock** (page 233)
Salt and pepper
One 1-pound squab
1 teaspoon peanut oil
One 4-ounce piece raw duck foie gras (see **NOTE**)
4 slices French bread
1 pinch sugar

PREPARATIONS:

Peel the turnips and carrots and then trim them into ovals about 1½ to 2 inches long. Trim the stems of the onions, leaving about 1 inch attached, and chop enough of the removed stems to make about 2 tablespoons. Separate the leaves of the cabbage and remove the central vein in each leaf. Peel the garlic cloves. Mince the shallot.

Start the base for the red-wine sauce by putting 1 tablespoon of the butter and the minced shallot in a small heavy saucepan. Cook over medium heat until the butter foams and then add the red wine and the veal stock and reduce over high heat until the liquid is thick enough to coat a spoon.

COOKING:

Season the white stock and bring it to a boil in a pan slightly larger than the squab. Lower the heat, add the squab, and poach it gently, without letting the stock boil, for 25 minutes. If the squab isn't completely covered by the stock, turn it over halfway through the cooking time.

While the squab is poaching, prepare the other ingredients. Cook the turnips, carrots, and onions together in enough salted water barely to cover, along with 1 tablespoon of the butter, until they are tender but still slightly firm. Cook the cabbage leaves for about 10 minutes in salted boiling water and drain them. Roll them together into a ball like a little cabbage and squeeze in a towel to remove all the water. Cook the garlic cloves in a small saucepan with the oil. When the garlic starts to brown, add 1 tablespoon of the butter, season with salt, and set aside.

About 5 minutes before the squab is done, add the piece of foie gras, whole, to the pan with the squab. Toast the bread slices. Finish the red-wine sauce by reheating it and then whisking in the remaining 3 tablespoons of butter. Season with salt, pepper, the pinch of sugar, and a few drops of red wine.

PRESENTATION:

Put the squab and the whole slice of foie gras in a soup tureen and arrange the vegetables around them. Pour the cooking broth into the tureen and sprinkle with the chopped onion green. Along with the tureen, present the sauce in a sauceboat and the toasted bread slices on a small plate, each topped with one of the garlic cloves and some of their butter.

To serve, remove the squab from the tureen, skin it, and cut in half. Put half the bird on each plate. Remove the foie gras, cut it in half diagonally, and put on the plates. Cut the little cabbage in half. Arrange all the vegetables around the squab and foie gras and coat the foie gras with the red-wine sauce. Serve the broth separately in bowls and pass the toast.

NOTE: *See page 30 for information on foie gras. The pot-au-feu will not be the same without the foie gras, but it certainly may be omitted. The red-wine sauce is excellent on the squab. Ed.*

Coeur de pigeon "Saint-François"

STUFFED SQUAB "HEARTS"

TO SERVE 4:

4 squabs, with their innards
⅓ pound sweetbreads
1 shallot
2 ounces fresh truffles (see page 31)
3 tablespoons butter
Salt and pepper
3½ ounces **Terrine of Duck Foie Gras** (see page 54 and
    page 55)
4 egg yolks
4 tablespoons madeira

PREPARATIONS:

Bone the squabs: For each one, first cut off the wing tips at the second joint. Put the squab in front of you with the breast down. You want to end up with a completely boned squab with the meat still attached to the skin and the skin still in one piece. This requires a combination of cutting and peeling. Start by making an incision down the back of the bird. Cut down to the tail and cut the tail off.

Now carefully peel and cut the meat and skin on the back away from the bone, first working down one side and then the other. Twist and cut through the joints holding each of the thighs and wings to the carcass so that the bones separate from the rest of the carcass. Turn the bird over and carefully separate the meat and skin on the breast from the bone. At this point, you can remove the carcass from the bird.

Now take each of the wings and thighs, one after the other, and turn it so that the joint that held it to the carcass points up. Peel and scrape the flesh and skin away from the bone, going from top to bottom. Remove the bone. Don't worry about getting all the meat off the drumstick bone before pulling it out. (Cut this meat off the drumstick bone and set it aside to use in the stuffing.)

When all the bones are removed, very carefully cut out and remove the central membrane between the two chunks of breast meat. Do this without cutting or breaking the skin. Set the boned birds aside until ready to stuff. The carcasses can be saved to make a little bouillon, or you can cook them with the squab "hearts." This isn't indispensable, but it can't help but improve the sauce.

Cut open the gizzards and skin them. Cut the gizzard meat into small dice. Cut the livers and hearts into medium-size dice and do the same with the meat from the squab legs set aside earlier. Cut the sweetbreads into ½-inch cubes. Chop the shallot and cut the truffles into fine dice.

Melt 2 tablespoons of the butter in a frying pan and sauté the sweetbreads for 1½ minutes over high heat, stirring constantly. Add the liver, heart, gizzard, and thigh meat, season, add the chopped shallot, and cook, still stirring, for another minute. Then add the truffle dice and the remaining 1 tablespoon of butter to the pan and cook another minute. Check the seasoning, remove from the heat, and let cool.

Purée half the cooled mixture with half the foie gras in a food processor or food mill, or force it through a fine strainer. Dice the rest of the foie gras. Mix together the puréed stuffing mixture, the stuffing that was not puréed, the diced foie gras, and the egg yolks. Check the seasoning.

Spread the boned birds out in front of you, skin side down. Put a quarter of the stuffing in the center of each breast. Pull each of the two bottom corners of the skin up to the top of the breast so that the bottom edges of the skin are aligned vertically in the center of the breast. Bring the top flap of skin down and sew the whole together to form a triangle or heart shape.

COOKING:

Heat the oven to 450°F. Salt and pepper the squab "hearts," put them in a lightly oiled baking dish over high heat, along with the bones if you are using them, and sear the "hearts" on both sides. Cook the seared birds in the preheated oven for 14 to 15 minutes. Baste them often and turn them after 7 minutes.

Remove from the oven and put the "hearts" on a warm serving platter or on individual plates. Put the madeira and ¼ cup water into the pan and scrape the bottom of the pan to get all the cooked-on juices into the sauce. Bring to a boil once or twice and then strain and check the seasoning.

PRESENTATION:

Remove the thread from the "hearts," turn them breast side up, and pour the sauce over them.

COMMENT: This was a specialty of my father.

viandes
et abats

MEATS &
VARIETY
MEATS

Mignonnette d'agneau
au persil et aux champignons

LAMB FILLETS WITH PARSLEY
AND MUSHROOMS

TO SERVE 4:

1 ⅓ pounds (about 7 large bunches) parsley
1 garlic clove
1 shallot
¾ pound wild mushrooms (see **NOTES**)
5 tablespoons butter
⅔ cup heavy cream
Salt and pepper
2 tablespoons peanut oil
Four 6-ounce lamb fillets, cut from the saddle (see **NOTES**)

PREPARATIONS:

Cut or twist the stems off the parsley. Blanch the leaves in salted boiling water for 6 minutes, squeeze well, and let dry on paper towels. Chop the garlic and the shallot. Clean the mushrooms and unless they are very small ones cut them into halves or quarters.

FINISHING:

Put 3 tablespoons of the butter into a frying pan with the chopped shallot. Cook over medium heat until the butter foams and then add the parsley. Stir it with a fork to separate. Add the cream and bring to a boil twice so that it thickens slightly and the parsley absorbs some of it. Season with salt and pepper, remove the pan from the heat, and set aside.

Heat 1 tablespoon of the oil in a non-stick frying pan over high heat and add the mushrooms. When they have yielded their juices, add the remaining 2 tablespoons of butter, the chopped garlic, and salt and pepper. Mix well and let cook, still over high heat, until the mushrooms are well browned. Remove from the heat and set aside.

Heat the remaining 1 tablespoon of oil in a frying pan over medium heat. Salt and pepper the lamb fillets and sauté for 4 minutes a side.

Cut the fillets into thin slices. Arrange the slices of each fillet on an individual plate in the shape of a star. Put the parsley in the center and scatter the mushrooms over the meat.

NOTES: *If fresh wild mushrooms are not available, the dish is still excellent made with a combination of ½ ounce dried wild mushrooms, reconstituted in warm water, and ½ pound cultivated fresh mushrooms.*

For this recipe you will need a whole saddle. Strip out both the loin sections, remove all the fat, and cut each strip of meat in half crosswise. Stand each piece on end and flatten with your hand and then smack it with the flat of a cleaver a couple of times to form it into a thick fillet. Ed.

Noisettes d'agneau
à la truffe et aux pommes lyonnaise

LAMB NOISETTES WITH TRUFFLES AND LYONNAISE POTATOES

TO SERVE 4:

1 small bunch parsley
3 ounces fresh truffles (see **NOTE**)
1 pound potatoes
1 small onion
1 egg yolk
Salt and pepper
Eight 1-inch-thick lamb noisettes, cut from the loin section of the
    saddle
3 tablespoons peanut oil
4 tablespoons butter
¼ cup **veal glaze** (page 234)

PREPARATIONS:

Mince enough parsley to make ½ cup. Mince the truffles. Mix the parsley with three quarters of the truffles. Peel the potatoes and cut them into slices about ⅛ inch thick. Cut the onions into thin slices and separate into rings. In a small bowl, mix the egg yolk with 1 teaspoon water as for a pastry glaze.

FINISHING:

Salt and pepper the lamb and then use a pastry brush to coat each piece with the egg glaze. Roll the lamb pieces in the parsley and truffle mixture, pressing firmly so that the mixture sticks to the noisettes. The Lyonnaise potatoes and the lamb should be cooked as nearly simultaneously as possible. You will need two frying pans, one of them a non-stick pan.

For the lamb, heat 1 tablespoon of the oil over high heat in the non-stick pan and add the noisettes. Let them cook 3 minutes, turning once. Add the butter and let the meat cook, off the heat, for 2 more minutes.

Meanwhile, start the potatoes by heating the remaining 2 tablespoons oil in a frying pan until very hot. Add the potatoes and cook them 5 minutes in all. Turn them often and add the onion rings to the pan after 2 minutes.

Remove the noisettes from their pan. Add the remaining minced truffle and the veal glaze to the pan, bring the sauce to a boil, and season with salt and pepper.

PRESENTATION:

Arrange the Lyonnaise potatoes in the centers of four plates and put the noisettes on top of them. Pour a band of sauce around the potatoes.

NOTE: *This is a memorable dish even without the truffles. Dip the noisettes in plain parsley and use a few flavorful dried mushrooms, reconstituted in warm water, in the sauce in place of the truffles. See page 31 for information on truffles.*

Selle d'agneau à la
graine de moutarde

SADDLE OF LAMB WITH
MUSTARD SEED SAUCE

TO SERVE 2:

1 shallot
1 sprig parsley
1 sprig chervil
1 blade chive
One 2-pound saddle of lamb, trimmed of fat and chined
Salt and pepper
1 tablespoon peanut oil
4 large garlic cloves
1 sprig thyme
1 sprig rosemary
6 tablespoons butter
2 tablespoons Dijon mustard
1 tablespoon mustard seeds

PREPARATIONS:

Mince the shallot and chop enough of the parsley, chervil, and chive to make ¼ teaspoon.

COOKING:

Heat the oven to 400°F. Season the lamb with salt and pepper. In a roasting pan, heat the oil over high heat. Set the saddle in the pan and add the garlic cloves, unpeeled, the thyme, and rosemary. Sear the saddle quickly on all sides. Put ½ tablespoon of the butter on the top and then put the roasting pan in the preheated oven for 20 minutes. While it is cooking, baste the lamb often, adding another ½ tablespoon of the butter twice.

Take the saddle out of the oven and place on a warm platter. Put 4 tablespoons of the butter on the saddle and let the lamb sit about 10 minutes, continuing to baste it often with the butter and juices on the platter. While the lamb is resting, deglaze the roasting pan by adding 2 tablespoons water, bringing to a boil, and scraping the bottom of the pan well to free all the cooked-on juices. Put through a strainer into a small saucepan, pressing the garlic out of its skins and through the strainer into the sauce. Keep warm.

When the saddle has rested 10 minutes, scrape all the butter from the platter into a small frying pan and add the minced shallot and the Dijon mustard. Cook over high heat, whisking continually, until the mustard becomes granular. Then add the remaining ½ tablespoon of butter, cook until it foams, and stir in the mustard seeds. Bring the sauce just to a boil and add the ¼ teaspoon herbs. Spread the mustard sauce over the saddle.

PRESENTATION:

Present the saddle on a platter and carve at the table. The deglazing juices should be served separately in a small sauceboat.

Noix de ris de veau au porto et aux câpres

SWEETBREADS WITH PORT AND CAPERS

TO SERVE 2:

2 lobes sweetbreads, about 1 pound in all (see **NOTE**)
Salt and pepper
A few drops oil
3 tablespoons butter
2 teaspoons capers
⅓ cup port
3 tablespoons **veal stock** (page 234)
¼ lemon

PREPARATIONS:

Put the sweetbreads in a bowl and set under running water for 3 to 4 hours. Using a small knife, cut and peel away the membrane and fat. Cut each lobe horizontally into 2 slices.

FINISHING:

Season the sweetbreads with salt and pepper. Heat a few drops oil in a non-stick frying pan over medium-high heat and then sear the sweetbreads 3 minutes per side. Reduce to low heat, add the butter to the pan, and baste the sweetbreads with the foaming butter for 2 minutes. Now add the capers, port, and veal stock. Increase the heat, squeeze 1 teaspoon of lemon juice into the pan, and bring the sauce just to a boil. Remove the pan from the heat, baste the sweetbreads several times with the sauce, and taste for seasoning.

PRESENTATION:

Put the sweetbreads on heated plates and pour the sauce over them.

NOTE: *The sweetbreads are not blanched before cooking. Ed.*

Émincé de veau à la fricassée
d'artichauts et petits pois

VEAL WITH ARTICHOKES AND LITTLE PEAS

TO SERVE 4:

1 pound veal round steak
8 cooked **artichoke bottoms** (page 239)
12 tablespoons butter
¾ pound little peas in their shells, about ½ cup shelled
1 sprig parsley
2 shallots
1 spring onion
1 tablespoon peanut oil
Salt and pepper
⅔ cup white wine

PREPARATIONS:

Cut the veal into strips ¼ inch thick, ½ inch wide, and 1 inch long. Cut the cooked artichoke bottoms into quarters and put them in a frying pan with ¼ cup of their cooking liquid and 4 tablespoons of the butter. Shell the peas and cook them in salted boiling water for 2 minutes and drain. Add them to the artichokes and set aside. Cut up a good pinch of parsley, chop the shallots, and slice the spring onion as thin as possible.

Heat the oil in a frying pan over high heat. Season the veal with salt and pepper and sauté for 30 seconds, stirring. Add the chopped shallots and 4 tablespoons of the butter to the frying pan and continue cooking and stirring for another 30 seconds. Remove the meat with a slotted spoon and set aside.

Add the wine to the pan, bring to a boil, and reduce over high heat for 2 minutes, scraping the bottom of the pan firmly. Add the sliced onion to the pan, remove from the heat, and thicken the sauce by whisking in the remaining 4 tablespoons of butter. Put the veal back in the pan with the sauce and set the pan on the edge of the burner to keep veal and sauce warm. They should not, however, continue to cook. Check the seasoning.

Reheat the vegetables over medium heat until the artichoke bottoms are glazed and golden.

PRESENTATION:

Put the veal strips in the center of warm plates and arrange the artichokes and peas around them. Sprinkle with the parsley.

COMMENT: This preparation is really an émincé de veau in the Zurich style, one of the most famous of Swiss specialties that does not, despite the way it is often prepared, contain cream.

Pièce de veau poêlée aux bettes

SAUTÉED VEAL STEAK WITH SWISS CHARD

TO SERVE 2:

2 shallots
4 ribs Swiss chard
½ cup red wine
¾ cup **veal stock** (page 234)
Salt and pepper
One ⅔-pound veal round steak, cut about ¾ inch thick
1 tablespoon peanut oil
3 tablespoons butter
1 tablespoon olive oil
1 pinch thyme
3 tablespoons heavy cream

PREPARATIONS:

Mince the shallots. Remove the leaves from the ribs of Swiss chard, cut out any especially large veins in the leaves and throw away, and then cut the leaves into 3 or 4 pieces each. Remove the strings from the ribs as you would from celery and then cut the ribs into ¼-inch slices. Blanch the leaves in salted boiling water for 3 minutes. Drain, squeeze gently to dry, chop, and set aside.

Start the red-wine sauce by putting half the shallots and all the wine in a saucepan and boiling until the liquid has the consistency of a thick syrup. Add the veal stock and reduce by one third over high heat. Taste for seasoning.

COOKING:

Cook the veal and the Swiss chard ribs at the same time. Salt and pepper the veal. Heat the peanut oil in a frying pan over medium heat and sauté the veal for about 7 minutes, turning at least once. Remove the meat from the frying pan and pour out the oil. Replace it with 1 tablespoon of the butter. Return the meat to the pan, add the remaining chopped shallots, and cook over low heat for about 3 minutes, basting the veal with the melted butter.

Heat the olive oil in another frying pan over high heat, add the chard ribs and the thyme, and sauté them for no more than 6 minutes so that the chard is cooked but still firm. Season with salt and pepper and add 1 tablespoon of the butter.

Put the chard leaves in a saucepan with the remaining 1 tablespoon of butter. Melt the butter over medium heat and then season with salt and pepper and add the cream. Let cook a few minutes at a gentle boil until the cream thickens.

Reheat the red-wine sauce and add the juices and butter from the veal to it.

PRESENTATION:

Arrange the chard ribs in a circle on a round, warmed serving platter or plates. Put the chard leaves and cream in the center of the circle. Cut the veal into ½-inch slices but keep them together in the original shape of the steak. Put the veal on top of the chard leaves. Moisten the meat with the red-wine sauce and serve the remaining sauce in a sauceboat.

Émincé de veau au curry

CURRIED VEAL

TO SERVE 4:

1 pound veal round steak
4 rounded teaspoons curry powder
Salt and pepper
A few drops peanut oil
2 tablespoons butter
⅔ cup white wine
1 ¼ cups heavy cream
½ lemon

PREPARATIONS:

Cut the veal into strips about ¼ inch thick, ½ inch wide, and 1 inch long.

FINISHING:

Put the veal strips on a platter or in a large bowl and sprinkle them with the curry powder (use somewhat less than called for if you prefer a lightly flavored curry). Salt and pepper the veal and mix the strips together with the seasonings, using your hands, to make sure all the meat is well flavored. Heat the oil in a non-stick frying pan over high heat until the pan is quite hot. Put the veal strips in the pan and separate them with a fork. After 30 seconds, add the butter and sauté the veal a minute with the strips spread out in the pan, not heaped together. Remove the veal with a slotted spoon and set aside while you make the sauce.

Add the white wine to the pan and reduce by two thirds over high heat. Add the cream and let it reduce until the sauce is thick enough to coat to the back of a spoon. Remove the pan from the heat, add the veal strips, and leave in the pan just long enough to reheat them but not to cook them any further. Check the seasoning, squeeze in about 1 teaspoon lemon juice, and serve immediately.

PRESENTATION:

You can garnish the veal with condiments such as toasted almonds and fried onion rings. It is good served with buttered rice topped with diced green peppers, raisins, and little peas.

Noisettes de veau à la hongroise

VEAL NOISETTES WITH PAPRIKA AND PEPPERS

TO SERVE 4:

1 ½ pounds veal tenderloin, cut into 12 slices
½ red bell pepper
3 sprigs parsley
Salt and pepper
4 teaspoons peanut oil
4 tablespoons butter
4 teaspoons sweet Hungarian paprika
1 dried red chili pepper, about ½ teaspoon crushed
⅓ cup water
1 cup heavy cream
¼ lemon
1 tablespoon sliced almonds

PREPARATIONS:

If the meat has not already been sliced by the butcher, cut it into 12 even slices, 1 to 1 ¼ inches thick. Remove the seeds and white interior ribs from the red bell pepper. Cut the pepper into ⅛-inch strips and then cut the strips into ⅛-inch dice. You'll need ¼ cup of dice. Chop enough parsley to make 1 tablespoon.

FINISHING:

Season the veal with salt and pepper. Heat 1 tablespoon of the peanut oil in a frying pan over medium heat. When the oil is quite hot, sear the veal noisettes in it for 1 minute, turning them once. Lower the heat and add the butter and the paprika. Cook until the butter starts to foam and then remove the veal slices and set them aside while you complete the sauce.

With the frying pan still over medium heat, add the dried red chili pepper and the water. Over high heat, bring to a boil several times, stirring each time to interrupt the boiling, to reduce the sauce, and then add the cream. Scrape the bottom of the pan to free any coagulated juices and let the sauce reduce over high heat until it is thick enough to coat the back of a spoon. Check the seasoning. The dish should be quite spicy.

Put the veal noisettes back in the pan along with the juices they've rendered while resting. Bring the sauce to a boil once more and remove from the heat. Season to taste with about 1 teaspoon lemon juice. Quickly sauté the diced pepper in a teaspoon of oil and drain.

PRESENTATION:

Serve the dish on warm plates. Put three noisettes in the center of each plate, sprinkle them with the red pepper dice, and coat them with the sauce. Garnish with the sliced almonds and chopped parsley.

Rognon de veau sauté à la Dôle

VEAL KIDNEY WITH RED-WINE SAUCE

TO SERVE 4:

2 large veal kidneys
3 shallots
1 cup red wine
1 ½ cups **veal stock** (page 234)
Salt and pepper
1 large pinch sugar
1 garlic clove
2 sprigs thyme
1 or 2 sprigs parsley
2 tablespoons olive oil
1 ⅓ cups fresh bread crumbs
4 tablespoons butter
A few drops eau-de-vie, such as kirsch

PREPARATIONS:

Pare the fat from the kidneys so that only a thin skin of fat is left. Save the fat parings. Cut the kidneys in half horizontally and remove any interior veins or pieces of skin that are visible. Put the pieces of pared fat on the bottom of a shallow baking pan just large enough to hold the kidney pieces comfortably. Put the kidneys on top of the fat and set aside.

Chop the shallots and put two thirds of them in a small heavy saucepan. Add the wine and cook over moderate heat until the wine reduces to the consistency of thick syrup. Add the veal stock and reduce by one third over high heat. Season with salt and pepper and the sugar. Set aside.

Chop the garlic, thyme, and enough parsley to make 2 teaspoons. In a small saucepan, heat the olive oil over low heat. Add the garlic, the remaining shallots, the thyme, and parsley. Stir continually for 1 minute and then add the bread crumbs. Remove from the heat and set aside.

FINISHING:

Heat the oven to 425°F. Season the kidney slices with salt and pepper and put them in the oven. Let the fat melt for about 5 minutes without opening the oven and then baste several times with the melted fat during the rest of the cooking. Turn the kidneys after they have cooked 7 minutes and remove them from the oven after 11 minutes in all. Now heat the broiler.

Lift the kidneys from the baking pan and let any blood drip into the saucepan of reduced wine and stock. Discard all the fat in the baking pan and return the kidneys to it. Cover them with the bread crumb mixture.

Reheat the red wine and stock reduction, remove from the heat, and whisk in the butter to thicken the sauce. Check the seasoning and add the eau-de-vie. Put the crumb-coated kidneys under the broiler for ½ minute to brown the topping lightly.

PRESENTATION:

Pour the sauce onto warm plates and put half a kidney in the middle of each plate.

Rognon de veau "Bolo"
SAUTÉED VEAL KIDNEY

TO SERVE 2:

1 top-quality veal kidney
2 teaspoons peanut oil
Salt and pepper
3 tablespoons butter

PREPARATIONS:

Trim the fat from the kidney so that only a thin, skin-like layer is left. Cut the kidney into slices about ¼ inch thick.

FINISHING:

Heat the oil over high heat in a heavy frying pan, preferably enameled cast iron. When the oil starts smoking, put the kidney slices in the pan. Season with salt and pepper, add the butter, turn the slices over, and remove the skillet from the burner. The whole process should take exactly 1 minute.

PRESENTATION:

Serve immediately on warm plates with the butter and oil poured over the kidney slices.

COMMENT: The success of this dish depends first on the quality of the veal kidney and secondly on the quickness of the cooking. Consequently if you are doubling the recipe to serve four people, it is preferable to serve it in two stages. First cook one kidney and serve and after eating it cook and serve the second one.

gibier
et lapin

GAME &
RABBIT

Perdreau en casserole aux
carottes glacées et au coulis de poireaux

PARTRIDGE WITH GLAZED CARROTS AND LEEKS

TO SERVE 2:

½ pound (about 5) carrots
1 small onion
2 large leeks
One ¾-pound partridge, with liver and heart
Salt and pepper
5 tablespoons butter
1 sprig thyme
3 tablespoons water
3 tablespoons heavy cream
1 ½ tablespoons champagne
⅓ cup **game stock** (page 236)

PREPARATIONS:

Peel the carrots and cut into thin diagonal slices. Chop the onion. Cut off and discard the dark green leaves from the leeks and wash the white and light-green sections. Slice them into quarters lengthwise and then cut crosswise into ½-inch pieces. Separate the layers. Set aside the liver and heart of the partridge, season the bird inside and out, and truss it.

COOKING:

Reserve 3 or 4 slices of carrot and ½ tablespoon onion. In a saucepan, melt ½ tablespoon of the butter over low heat and cook the remaining onions until they soften. Add the remaining carrots and cook over medium heat a few minutes until they begin to brown. Add water to half cover, reduce heat to low, and cook, covered, for 20 minutes, until the carrots are glazed.

Melt 2 tablespoons of the butter in a heavy flameproof casserole. Put the partridge in the casserole on its side. Add the liver, the heart, the reserved slices of carrot and ½ tablespoon of onion, ½ tablespoon of the leeks, and the thyme. Cook the partridge gently over medium heat for 5 minutes, turn to the other side, and cook another 5 minutes. Then turn the bird on its back for a final 10 minutes cooking. After 5 minutes cooking on its back, pour off the browned butter in the casserole and replace it with 2 tablespoons of fresh butter. Baste the breasts of the partridge several times during the final 5 minutes of cooking.

While the partridge is cooking, season the remaining leeks and sauté them over high heat in ½ tablespoon of the butter for 2 minutes. Add the water to moisten and then cook until the water completely evaporates. Add the cream and continue cooking, still over high heat, for 1 minute, or until the cream thickens and coats the leeks. Remove from the heat and set aside until ready to serve.

When the partridge has cooked for 20 minutes, remove it to a warm plate and remove the trussing strings. Cut the bird in half and cut out the backbone. Put the bone in the casserole and set the casserole over medium-high heat. Add the champagne, bring to a boil, and scrape the bottom of the casserole to incorporate any cooked-on juices into the liquid. Add the game stock and continue to boil for 2 minutes. Strain.

PRESENTATION:

Put the leeks in the middle of heated plates and the partridge halves on top of them. Arrange the carrots in a semicircle on the top half of each plate. Coat the partridge with the sauce.

Aile de poule
faisane aux radis noirs

PHEASANT BREASTS WITH BLACK RADISHES

TO SERVE 2:

1 pound black radishes (see **NOTE** page 188)
3½ tablespoons butter
3 tablespoons **game stock** (page 236)
3 tablespoons port
3 tablespoons white wine
Salt and pepper
¼ lemon
10 peppercorns
One 2-pound pheasant

PREPARATIONS:

Peel the radishes. Cut them into pieces and then pare the corners so that each piece is about the size of a garlic clove. Melt 1 ½ tablespoons of the butter in a saucepan over medium heat. Add the radishes and cook 5 to 6 minutes, stirring, to brown. Discard excess butter from the pan and add the game stock, port, wine, and salt and pepper to the radishes. Cook about 15 minutes, or until the radishes are tender and the liquid is syrupy. If it is too thick and sticks to the pan, add a bit of water but not too much, since there should be about 6 to 8 tablespoons of liquid in the pan, no more. Check the seasoning, squeeze in ¼ teaspoon lemon juice, and set aside.

Crush the peppercorns in a mortar with a pestle.

Only the breast and wings are used in this dish. Make an incision along the breast-bone and then, with the blade against the bones so that you get all the meat, cut down, removing the breast until you reach the wing joint. Cut through the joint connecting the wing to the carcass and take off the wing and breast meat in one piece. Cut off the wing tip leaving one joint on the breast. Repeat for the other side of the pheasant.

COOKING:

Heat the oven to 550°F. In a baking dish just large enough to hold the breasts without overlapping, cook the remaining 2 tablespoons of butter over medium heat until lightly browned. Season the pheasant breasts and put them in the baking dish, skin side down. Open the oven door and set the dish on the door, just at the entrance to the oven. Cook them about 15 minutes, turning once and basting continuously with the butter. Meanwhile, reheat the radishes. Remove the breasts from the dish when they are still pink and juicy. Cut the breast meat into 5 or 6 slices, which should remain attached at the wing.

PRESENTATION:

Serve on warm plates with the wing at the bottom and the slices spread out like a fan. Arrange the radishes in an arc above the pheasant and coat them with their sauce. Sprinkle the radishes with the crushed pepper.

Émincé de lapin à la moutarde

RABBIT IN MUSTARD SAUCE

TO SERVE 3 TO 4:

Back legs and front leg section from a 3- to 3½-pound domestic
  rabbit (see **COMMENT**)
1 small shallot
Salt and pepper
3 tablespoons butter
4 teaspoons mild mustard
⅓ cup white wine
1 teaspoon **veal stock** (page 234)
⅓ cup heavy cream

PREPARATIONS:

Bone the rabbit, remove the tendons, and cut the meat into strips about ¾ inch long and
⅓ inch wide. This should be about 1 pound of meat. Put it in a bowl to catch any juices.
Chop the shallot.

FINISHING:

Season the rabbit strips with salt and pepper. Heat the butter in a frying pan over medium
heat. Add the shallot and the rabbit strips, reserving the rabbit juices in the bowl, and stir
for about 2 minutes. Remove the meat from the pan and keep warm.

Add 3 teaspoons of the mustard, the wine, and the veal stock to the frying pan. Mix
together well, scrape the bottom of the pan to deglaze, and then reduce the liquid by two
thirds over high heat until the sauce lightly coats the back of a spoon. Add the cream to the
reduced liquid and let it cook over high heat until the liquid in the pan is again reduced,
this time by at least half. Remove the pan from the heat and add to the sauce the rabbit
juices that you set aside earlier and the remaining 1 teaspoon of mustard. Mix well, put
the rabbit slices back in the pan with the sauce, and reheat without boiling. Check the
seasoning and serve.

COMMENT: The saddle of the rabbit can be used to prepare **Saddle of Rabbit with
Basil** (following recipe). The liver and kidneys can be used for **Rabbit Tidbits with
Morels and Black Truffles** (page 79) or the liver for **Rabbit Liver and Leeks in
Puff Pastry** (page 78).

Râble de lapin au basilic

SADDLE OF RABBIT WITH BASIL

TO SERVE 2:

1 bouquet basil
3 shallots
The saddle from a domestic rabbit weighing about 3½ pounds
    (see **COMMENT**, preceding recipe)
Salt and pepper
1 tablespoon peanut oil
4 garlic cloves
¼ cup white wine or **chicken stock** (page 232)
1 tablespoon **veal stock** (page 234)
2 tablespoons butter

PREPARATIONS:

Cut enough basil leaves to make 2 heaping tablespoons of strips. Cut the shallots into quarters. Trim the rabbit and then make two deep incisions, one on each side of the backbone from one end to the other. Stuff half of the basil into the incisions.

COOKING:

Heat the oven to 350°F. Season the rabbit with salt and pepper. Heat the oil in a frying pan. Put the rabbit, the garlic, unpeeled, and the shallots in the pan. Turn the rabbit so that each side just loses its red color. Do this quickly; remember you're not cooking the rabbit at this point.

    Put the rabbit, shallots, oil, and garlic in a flameproof baking dish and cook for 12 minutes in the preheated oven. Baste and turn the rabbit often and watch to see that it does *not* brown. Turn off the oven, remove the rabbit, put it on another baking dish, and set it back in the oven with the heat turned off while you finish the sauce.

    Pour the wine and veal stock into the first baking dish and bring to a boil, scraping the bottom to incorporate any cooked-on juices. Let cook several minutes over medium heat until the garlic and shallots are soft. Strain into a small saucepan. Squeeze the garlic out of its skins and push as much of it and the shallots through the strainer as possible. Bring the sauce back to a boil to reduce it a little. Add the rest of the basil to the pan and thicken the sauce by whisking the butter into it. Season with salt and pepper.

Remove the meat from the bone and slice the saddle lengthwise (with the grain). Arrange the slices on plates and pour the sauce over them. The dish is good served with a vegetable purée and a **Potato Paillasson** (page 185).

Râble de lièvre en
aiguillettes aux poires Curé

SADDLE OF WILD RABBIT WITH PEARS

TO SERVE 4:

2 pears
¾ cup red wine
1 tablespoon sugar
1 cinnamon stick
1 bay leaf
3 peppercorns
Pepper sauce (page 238)
2 tablespoons butter
The saddle from a 4½-pound wild rabbit
Salt and pepper
½ tablespoon peanut oil

PREPARATIONS:

Prepare the pears in red wine, if possible, the day before serving so that they will take on a lovely deep-red color. Peel the pears, cut them in half, and remove their cores with a melon baller. Put them in a saucepan. Set aside 2 tablespoons of the red wine and pour the rest over the pears. Add the sugar, cinnamon, bay leaf, and peppercorns.

Drape a piece of aluminum foil over the pears and set an inverted plate slightly smaller than the pan on top of the foil to keep the pears submerged in the wine. Simmer until tender, about 20 minutes or longer, depending on the firmness of the pears. Remove the pan from the heat and let the pears macerate either refrigerated or at room temperature.

Prepare the pepper sauce but don't whisk in the final tablespoons of butter.

COOKING:

Heat the oven to 500°F. Reheat the pears gently in their sauce and then drain them. Put them in a frying pan with 1 tablespoon of the butter and the reserved 2 tablespoons red wine. Cook briefly over medium heat to reduce the wine so that the pears are lightly glazed.

Season the rabbit saddle with salt and pepper. Heat the oil in a roasting pan over medium-high heat. Add the saddle and brown lightly on both sides. Put the saddle in the preheated oven and cook 6 minutes in all, turning it so that both sides are evenly exposed to the heat. After 6 minutes, remove the pan from the oven but leave the oven on. Pour off the oil in the pan and replace it with the remaining 1 tablespoon of butter. Make two deep cuts in the rabbit meat, one along each side of the backbone.

Open the oven door and set the pan with the saddle in it on the door right at the entrance to the oven. Baste continuously with the butter for 6 to 7 minutes while the saddle finishes cooking. When done, the meat near the bone should be rare. If you wish, you can cook the saddle a few minutes extra, but still on the oven door rather than in the oven.

Reheat the pepper sauce and whisk in the butter to thicken it as directed in the basic recipe.

PRESENTATION:

With a knife, remove the fillets from the saddle and then slice them lengthwise (with the grain). Divide the slices among four warm plates and coat with the pepper sauce. Garnish each plate with half a glazed pear and, if you wish, some **Swiss Egg Noodles** (page 181).

Noisettes de chevreuil poêlées
au chou rouge et aux châtaignes

SAUTÉED VENISON NOISETTES WITH RED CABBAGE AND CHESTNUTS

TO SERVE 4:

12 wild chestnuts (see **NOTES** page 174)
4 teaspoons sugar
⅓ cup water
⅓ cup **veal stock** (page 234)
½ rib celery
1 pound red cabbage
1 onion
1 garlic clove
1 shallot
1 apple
1 tablespoon red-wine vinegar
3 tablespoons butter
Salt and pepper
⅓ pound wild mushrooms
5 teaspoons peanut oil
Twelve 1-inch-thick venison noisettes cut from the tenderloin,
    about 1⅓ pounds in all

PREPARATIONS:

Shell and peel the chestnuts as in the glazed chestnut recipe (page 174). Put the sugar in a saucepan over low heat until it melts and turns a light caramel color. Immediately add the water and the veal stock and mix together until the caramel dissolves. Now add the celery and the chestnuts and continue cooking, covered, over low heat, stirring occasionally, until the chestnuts are tender and the liquid is quite syrupy, about 30 minutes. Add more water if needed so that the glaze doesn't burn. Remove and discard the celery and set the chestnuts aside.

Cut the cabbage into thin strips about ¼ inch wide and 1 inch long. Chop the onion, garlic, and shallot. Peel the apple, cut it into thin pieces like the cabbage strips, and toss with the vinegar. Melt 1 tablespoon of the butter over medium heat, add the chopped onion, and cook for 1 minute. Add the cabbage and cook until it begins to soften, about

5 minutes. Add water to come halfway up the cabbage. Now add the apple, season, and cook, covered, over low heat for about 30 to 35 minutes, depending on the freshness of the cabbage. Set aside.

Clean the mushrooms and if they are small leave them whole. Otherwise cut them in half. Large mushrooms can be quartered or even sliced.

FINISHING:

Reheat the cabbage and the chestnuts separately over low heat. At the same time, heat 1 tablespoon of the oil in a frying pan over high heat. Put the mushrooms in and sauté them until their rendered juices evaporate. Then add 1 tablespoon of the butter, the chopped garlic and shallot, and salt and pepper. Mix well and continue to cook for a couple of minutes until everything is nicely browned.

Season the noisettes with salt and pepper. Heat the remaining 2 teaspoons of oil in another frying pan over high heat. Sauté the venison for 1 minute, turn the noisettes, add the remaining 1 tablespoon of butter, and sauté them for another minute.

PRESENTATION:

Serve on warm plates. Arrange three chestnuts on one side of each plate, a quarter of the cabbage on the other, and three noisettes in the center. Scatter the sautéed mushrooms over the meat.

légumes et garnitures

VEGETABLES & GARNISHES

NOTE: *Many recipes in this chapter have appeared before as integral parts of other recipes in the book. Their manner of cooking is repeated here so that you may also use them independently.*

GREEN CABBAGE

TO SERVE 4:

20 leaves savoy cabbage
6 slices bacon
2 spring onions (see page 31)
3 tablespoons butter
Salt and pepper

PREPARATIONS:

Bring a large pot of salted water to a boil. Choose 20 nice, big leaves from a head of savoy cabbage, cut out their central ribs, and blanch the leaves for 1 minute in the boiling water. Refresh them under cold water and then drain them thoroughly. Cut each cabbage leaf into 4 or 5 pieces. Slice the bacon crosswise into thin julienne strips about ⅛-inch wide. Chop the onions fine.

FINISHING:

Put the butter in a large frying pan over low heat and add the bacon and onions. Cook until the butter becomes frothy and then add the cabbage and salt and pepper. Mix well and cook, still over low heat, 8 to 10 minutes. This is enough time to heat the vegetables through and to render their juices. Taste for seasoning.

This vegetable garnish is used in **Squab with Cabbage** (page 139).

Émincé de chou rouge

RED CABBAGE AND APPLE

TO SERVE 4:

1 pound red cabbage
1 onion
1 apple
1 tablespoon red-wine vinegar
3 tablespoons butter
Salt and pepper

PREPARATIONS:

Cut the cabbage into thin strips ¼ inch thick and 1 ¼ inches long. Chop the onion. Peel the apple, cut it into thin pieces like the cabbage, and toss with the vinegar. Melt the butter in a saucepan over medium heat, add the onion, cook for 1 minute, and add the cabbage strips. Cook, stirring, until the cabbage softens a bit, about 5 minutes. Add water to come halfway up the cabbage. Stir in the apple and salt and pepper and cook, covered, over low heat for 30 minutes. Adjust seasoning as needed.

FINISHING:

Reheat the cabbage, if necessary, over low heat and serve.

This vegetable garnish is used in **Sautéed Venison Noisettes with Red Cabbage and Chestnuts** (page 167).

GLAZED CARROTS

TO SERVE 4:

1¾ pounds (about 16) carrots
2 onions
3 tablespoons butter
Salt and pepper

PREPARATIONS:

Slice the carrots thin on the diagonal. Chop the onions.

COOKING:

In a saucepan, cook the onions with the butter over low heat until they're softened and then add the carrots. Raise the heat to medium, season the vegetables with salt and pepper, and cook until they color lightly. Add water to half cover them, reduce the heat to low, and let them cook, covered, for about 20 minutes. Adjust seasoning as needed.

This vegetable garnish is used in **Partridge with Glazed Carrots and Leeks** (page 160).

Châtaignes fondantes

GLAZED CHESTNUTS

TO SERVE 4:

20 wild chestnuts (see **NOTES**)
2 tablespoons sugar
½ cup water
½ rib celery
½ cup **veal stock** (page 234)
Salt and pepper

PREPARATIONS:

Of the different ways of shelling and peeling chestnuts, I think the following is the quickest and simplest: Heat to 350°F enough deep fat to cover the chestnuts. Cut a cross in the top of each shell and then plunge the chestnuts into the hot fat for a few seconds until the shells open at the cross. Peel them while still warm. The shells come off quite easily, and the skin can also be easily removed just by rubbing the chestnuts in a towel. (See **NOTES**.)

Put the sugar in a pan over low heat. Cook the sugar until it melts and turns a light caramel color and then immediately add ½ cup water and the veal stock and mix together until the caramel dissolves. Now add the celery, cut in thirds, and the chestnuts and continue cooking, covered, over low heat, stirring only occasionally, until chestnuts are tender and the liquid is quite syrupy, about 30 minutes. Add more water while cooking if needed so that the glaze doesn't burn. Remove and discard the celery.

FINISHING:

Reheat, if necessary, over low heat just before serving.

NOTES: *The most common method to loosen the shells from chestnuts is immersing in boiling water for 4 to 5 minutes. Fredy Girardet suggests a quick dip in deep fat rather than water. It works because the oil can be heated to a point considerably higher than the boiling point of water, and the higher heat more effectively separates the shells from the nut.*

Châtaignes are wild chestnuts still found in markets in France and Switzerland but rarely sold in this country. They are smaller and, in some varieties, more flavorful than cultivated chestnuts, but the latter can be substituted in this recipe. You may want to reduce the number of chestnuts to 12 or so, however, and increase the cooking time to about 45 minutes. Ed.

This vegetable garnish is used in **Sautéed Venison Noisettes with Red Cabbage and Chestnuts** (page 167).

Charlotte d'aubergines et
courgettes aux foies de volailles

EGGPLANT AND ZUCCHINI MOLDS WITH CHICKEN LIVERS

TO SERVE 4:

2 large eggplants
1 tablespoon butter
1 medium zucchini, about ¼ pound
4 spring onions (see page 31)
4 garlic cloves
1 sprig parsley
2½ tablespoons olive oil
2 ounces each chicken livers and hearts
Salt and pepper

PREPARATIONS:

With a vegetable peeler, remove the skin from the eggplants in wide strips. Blanch the skins for 30 seconds in salted boiling water. Drain them and then put in a frying pan with the butter and cook over high heat for about 30 seconds.

Butter four ½-cup molds (ideally 2⅓ inches in diameter and 1½ inches high). Line the molds with the bands of eggplant skin so that when unmolded the black side of the skin will be on the outside of the charlotte. Position each strip with one end in the center and the other hanging about 1 inch over the edge of the mold. Put a rectangular piece of skin in the bottom of the mold, if necessary, to mask any gaps.

Cut the zucchini and ¼ pound of the eggplant into ⅛-inch dice. You should have approximately equal quantities of zucchini and eggplant. Use the rest of the eggplant in another recipe. Chop the onions, garlic, and enough parsley to make 1 teaspoon. In a frying pan, heat 1½ tablespoons of the olive oil over medium heat. Add the garlic and onions and cook, without browning, just long enough to soften, about 3 minutes. Add the diced eggplant and zucchini and the remaining 1 tablespoon of olive oil to the frying pan, season with salt and pepper, and continue cooking over medium heat for 3 more minutes. Remove the pan from the heat and set aside.

Chop the chicken livers and hearts, season them with salt and pepper, and add them and the chopped parsley to the pan with the vegetables. Mix together and then spoon the mixture into the lined molds. Fill the molds completely, packing the vegetables down with the back of a spoon or a spatula, and then fold the ends of the eggplant strips back over the mixture. Push down with the palm of your hand to make the molds as compact as possible.

COOKING:

Heat the oven to 475°F. Put the molds in a water bath that comes about ⅓ up the sides of the molds. Bring the water to a boil on top of the stove and then slide the water bath into the preheated oven and cook the molds for 20 minutes.

PRESENTATION:

Unmold the charlottes and serve warm. They're particularly good with lamb.

ENDIVES WITH LEMON

TO SERVE 4:

1 lemon
2 pounds Belgian endives
1 tablespoon sugar
Salt and pepper
3 tablespoons butter

PREPARATIONS:

Squeeze the lemon. You'll need 3 tablespoons juice. Cut each endive on the diagonal, giving it a quarter turn after each cut so that you get triangular pieces. Separate the leaves and put them in a bowl.

FINISHING:

Season the endives with the sugar, 3 pinches of salt, 10 turns of the peppermill, and lemon juice and mix carefully by hand. Heat half the butter in each of two non-stick frying pans, put half the cut-up endives in each pan, and cook them over high heat for 3 minutes, stirring two or three times. Cook no longer or they will become soft and over-done. This is also the reason that you must not cook more than a pound of them in one frying pan, no matter how large. The endives must have plenty of room and high heat so that they'll cook quickly. Adjust seasoning as needed and serve.

This vegetable garnish is used in **Braised Chicken with Endives and Green Peppercorns** (page 130).

GNOCCHI PIEDMONT STYLE

TO SERVE 4:

¾ pound potatoes
Salt and pepper
Nutmeg
1 teaspoon olive oil
1 small bouquet mixed herbs (such as chervil, parsley, and basil)
1 egg yolk
¾ cup flour

PREPARATIONS:

Boil the potatoes, unpeeled, in salted water for 30 minutes, or until cooked through. Peel them while still warm and then put them through a food mill or push through a sieve to purée them. Mold the purée in a dome shape on a floured work surface and then make a well in the center of the dome. Season the purée with a pinch of salt and some pepper and a grating of nutmeg. Pour the olive oil over the surface of the dome and let sit until lukewarm.

Chop enough of the mixed herbs to make 2 tablespoons. Beat the egg yolk with a fork. When the potato purée is lukewarm, put the flour, beaten egg yolk, and the herbs into the well in the middle of the dome and work them gently into the dough with your fingers. Press the dough into a ball and knead it vigorously for a couple of minutes. Let rest for 10 minutes.

Cut the dough into 2 equal parts. Reflour the work surface and roll each half of the dough into a long cylinder about ¾ inch in diameter. Cut each roll into pieces ⅓ inch long. You can press each of the pieces against the prongs of a fork to give it a decorative fluting, but this is not mandatory.

COOKING:

Cook the gnocchi in a large pan of salted boiling water until they bob to the surface. Remove them as they surface and set them aside to drain.

PRESENTATION:

The gnocchi can be served as they are, accompanied by a tomato-herb sauce; or they can be sautéed lightly in butter and sprinkled with Parmesan; or they can be arranged in a gratin dish, coated with cream, and broiled until brown and bubbly.

LEEKS VAUDOISE

TO SERVE 4:

4 large leeks
3 tablespoons butter
⅓ cup water
⅓ cup heavy cream
Salt and pepper

PREPARATIONS:

Cut off and discard the dark green leaves from the leeks. Wash the white and light-green sections. Slice them into quarters lengthwise, cut them crosswise into ½-inch-long pieces, and separate the layers.

FINISHING:

In a frying pan, melt 2 tablespoons of the butter over high heat, add the leeks, and cook, stirring, for 2 minutes. Add the water and continue to cook over high heat until the water evaporates. Now add the cream and stir for 1 minute so that the cream thickens and coats the leeks. Season with salt and pepper to taste and add the remaining 1 tablespoon of butter.

This vegetable garnish is used in **Chicken Breasts with Leeks and Truffles** (page 126), in **Partridge with Glazed Carrots and Leeks** (page 160), and in **Rabbit Liver and Leeks in Puff Pastry** (page 78).

Fricassée de cèpes

WILD MUSHROOM FRICASSEE

TO SERVE 4:

1 ¼ pounds cèpes (see **NOTE**)
4 shallots
1 garlic clove
1 tablespoon peanut oil
3 tablespoons butter
Salt and pepper

PREPARATIONS:

Trim and clean the mushrooms, and cut them into thin slices. Mince the shallots and garlic.

FINISHING:

In a frying pan, heat the oil over high heat, add the mushrooms, and cook quickly just until their juices evaporate and they brown lightly. Add the butter, the chopped shallots, garlic, and salt and pepper, and brown for 1 minute. Remove the mixture from the pan and serve immediately.

NOTE: *This is a good recipe to use whenever any kind of fresh wild mushrooms are available. Ed.*

Spätzli

SWISS EGG NOODLES

TO SERVE 4 TO 6:

2 ¼ cups flour
5 eggs
⅔ cup milk
½ teaspoon salt
Pepper
Nutmeg
1 tablespoon peanut oil
4 tablespoons butter

PREPARATIONS:

Beat the flour and eggs together in a bowl until the mixture is smooth. Add the milk, season with the salt, pepper to taste, and a few gratings of nutmeg, and mix well.

Bring a large pot of water to a boil. Have ready a bowl of cold water. Hold a grater with openings about ⅜ inch in diameter over the pot of water and, with a plastic pastry scraper or spatula, scrape the dough, a little at a time, over the grater so that the batter goes through it into the boiling water. As the noodles rise to the surface of the water, remove them with a slotted spoon and put them into the bowl of cold water. Continue, alternately scraping the batter through the grater and letting it fall into the pan and removing the cooked noodles, until all are done. Drain the noodles well and combine with the oil so that they will not stick together.

FINISHING:

Melt the butter in a frying pan over medium-high heat, add the noodles, and sauté until golden brown. Season with salt and pepper and serve.

PRESENTATION:

These noodles are an accompaniment for game dishes, stews, and sautés.

ONION COMPOTE

TO SERVE 4 TO 6:

1 pound (3 to 4) onions
¼ cup red-wine vinegar, plus a few drops for finishing
1½ cups red wine
1½ cups water
3 tablespoons butter
2 tablespoons honey
Salt and pepper

PREPARATIONS:

Slice the onions. Put them in a pan with the vinegar and the wine. They should be just covered with the liquid. Cook over low heat, uncovered, until the liquid is completely absorbed, 30 to 45 minutes. Now add the water and continue cooking over low heat for 30 minutes, checking occasionally to see that the onions don't stick to the bottom of the pan. The onions are done when they are tender and juicy and have melted together. Now add the butter, honey, and salt and pepper, mix well, and set aside.

FINISHING:

Reheat the compote over low heat, check the seasoning, and add several drops of vinegar.

This vegetable garnish is used in **John Dory with Onion Compote and Tomato Butter** (page 93).

Persil en légume

PARSLEY WITH CREAM

TO SERVE 4:

2⅔ pounds (about 14 large bunches) parsley (see **NOTE**)
1 large shallot
4 tablespoons butter
1⅓ cup heavy cream
Salt and pepper

PREPARATIONS:

Cut or twist the large stems off the parsley and discard or save for bouquet garni. Bring a large pot of salted water to a boil. Add the parsley, bring back to a boil, and let it boil for 6 minutes. Drain it well, pressing with the back of a spoon. When it has cooled enough to handle, squeeze dry by handfuls and spread out on paper towels. Mince the shallot.

FINISHING:

Put the minced shallot and the butter in a frying pan. Cook over medium heat and when the butter starts to foam add the parsley. Stir it with a fork to separate. Add the cream and bring to a boil twice so it thickens slightly and the parsley absorbs some of it. Season the parsley with salt and pepper and serve as a vegetable.

NOTE: *This is not too much parsley to serve as a vegetable, but if you can't buy parsley cheaply in quantity, you might want to use half the recipe, which makes a nice small garnish for four. Ed.*

This vegetable is used as a garnish in **Lamb Fillets with Parsley and Mushrooms** (page 146).

PEARS IN RED WINE

TO SERVE 4:

4 pears
1 ½ cups red wine
2 tablespoons sugar
1 cinnamon stick
1 bay leaf
6 peppercorns
2 tablespoons butter

PREPARATIONS:

Peel the pears, cut them in half, and remove their cores with a melon baller. Put the cored pears in a saucepan so they fit snugly just touching one another. Set aside 3 tablespoons of the wine and pour the rest over the pears. Add the sugar, cinnamon, bay leaf, and pepper to the saucepan.

Drape a piece of aluminum foil over the pears and set an inverted plate slightly smaller than the pan on top of the foil to keep the pears submerged in the wine. Simmer until tender, about 20 minutes or longer, depending on the firmness of the pears. Remove the pan from the heat and let the pears macerate in the wine overnight, either refrigerated or at room temperature, so that they take on a lovely deep-red color.

FINISHING:

Reheat the pears gently in their sauce and then drain them. Put the pears in a frying pan with the butter and the reserved 3 tablespoons red wine. Cook briefly over medium heat to reduce the wine so that the pears are lightly glazed.

This fruit garnish is used in **Saddle of Wild Rabbit with Pears** (page 165).

Paillasson de pommes de terre

POTATO CAKE

TO SERVE 4:

1 ½ pounds potatoes
1 tablespoon peanut oil
Salt and pepper

PREPARATIONS:

Shred the potatoes into long strips. (**NOTE:** *The shredding blade of a food processor does this perfectly. Ed.*) Drain, pressing lightly to extract excess liquid.

COOKING:

Heat the oil over moderate heat in a non-stick pan. When it's hot, add the potatoes. Season them, stir well, and then let cook 10 minutes to brown and form a crust. Turn out onto a plate, slide back into the pan, and cook for 10 minutes on the second side. Cut into quarters and serve immediately.

Purée de pommes
nouvelles à l'huile d'olive

MASHED NEW POTATOES WITH OLIVE OIL

TO SERVE 4:

¾ pound new potatoes
¼ cup heavy cream
¼ cup olive oil
Salt and pepper
1 large pinch cayenne

Peel the potatoes and cook in salted boiling water until tender. Remove and push through a potato ricer or a sieve into a saucepan. Add the cream and whisk over medium heat until the cream is absorbed.

Still over medium heat, add the olive oil and stir it in with a wooden spoon. Then whisk for a few seconds to make sure the oil is completely absorbed. Season with salt, pepper, and the cayenne.

PRESENTATION:

Serve this purée as an accompaniment for fish, shellfish, and other dishes with the flavors of the south of France.

Pommes lyonnaise

LYONNAISE POTATOES

TO SERVE 4:

1 pound new potatoes
1 onion
2 tablespoons peanut oil
Salt and pepper

PREPARATIONS:

Peel the potatoes and slice them ⅛ inch thick. Cut the onion into thin slices and separate into rings.

FINISHING:

Heat the oil in a large frying pan. Season the potatoes and onion with salt and pepper, put the potatoes in the frying pan, and sauté them over high heat, turning them often, for 2 minutes. Then add the onion rings, continue cooking for 3 more minutes, stirring continually, and serve.

This vegetable garnish is used in **Lamb Noisettes with Truffles and Lyonnaise Potatoes** (page 147).

POTATO GRATIN GIRARDET

TO SERVE 4:

1 pound potatoes
1 small garlic clove
¾ cup milk
Salt and pepper
1 pinch cayenne
Nutmeg
6 tablespoons heavy cream
1 ½ tablespoons butter

PREPARATIONS:

Peel the potatoes and cut them into slices ⅛ inch thick. Do not wash the slices. Mince the garlic and mix it in with the potato slices. Put the potatoes and garlic in a heavy pan or flameproof casserole with just enough of the milk to cover the potatoes. Season with salt, pepper, cayenne, and a few gratings of nutmeg.

Put the pan over high heat and let the potatoes cook for 4 or 5 minutes, until the milk has made a liaison with the potato starch. Then add 3 tablespoons of the cream and bring the contents of the pan to a boil again. Remove from the heat and adjust the seasoning if needed.

Butter a 9½-inch gratin dish. Put in the potatoes and the cooking liquid and then add the rest of the cream, mixing it in with your hands to make sure it penetrates. Dot the butter over the surface.

COOKING:

Preheat the oven to 325°F. Bake the gratin on the bottom shelf of the oven for 1½ hours and serve.

BLACK RADISHES IN PORT
AND WINE SAUCE

TO SERVE 4:

2 pounds black radishes (see **NOTE**)
3 tablespoons butter
⅓ cup port
⅓ cup white wine
⅓ cup **veal stock** (page 234) or **game stock** (page 236;
    see also **COMMENT**)
Salt and pepper
¼ lemon

PREPARATIONS:

Peel the radishes. Cut them into pieces and then pare the corners so that each piece is about the size of a large garlic clove. Melt the butter in a saucepan over medium heat. Add the radishes and cook for 5 to 6 minutes, stirring, to brown. Pour off any excess butter. Add the port, the wine, and the stock, season with salt and pepper, and cook about 15 minutes, until the radishes are tender and the juice is syrupy. If you think the juice is too thick, add a bit of water but not too much since there should only be about 2 tablespoons of juice per serving. Check the seasoning and squeeze in lemon juice to taste, about ¼ teaspoon.

FINISHING:

Reheat the radishes, if necessary, over low heat and serve.

COMMENT: When serving the radishes with game, use the appropriate stock. Otherwise, use veal stock.

NOTE: *Black radishes are large and mild. They are available in winter and spring in Oriental markets. Ed.*

This vegetable garnish is used in **Pheasant Breasts with Black Radishes** (page 161).

SAUTÉED SALSIFY

TO SERVE 4:

8 salsify (oyster root or oyster plant), about ¾ pound in all
2 tablespoons peanut oil
Salt and pepper
2 tablespoons butter

PREPARATIONS:

Trim and peel the salsify and cut into small sticks about 1 inch long and ¼ inch wide.

COOKING:

Heat the oil in a frying pan over medium-high heat, add the salsify, and cook for 2 minutes, stirring constantly. Reduce the heat to medium and continue cooking for 5 minutes, turning the salsify occasionally and reducing the heat if it threatens to burn. Season the salsify, add the butter, and finish cooking over low heat until tender, 5 to 8 minutes.

This vegetable garnish is used in **Roast Duck with Salsify** (page 134).

BUTTERED NEW TURNIPS

TO SERVE 4:

32 very small new turnips with greens, about 2 pounds in all
Salt and pepper
2 tablespoons butter

PREPARATIONS:

Cut off the ends of the turnip greens, leaving 2½ inches attached to the root. Peel the turnips neatly, trimming off all the peeling in vertical strips. Protect the greens of each turnip by wrapping them in a small piece of aluminum foil.

Cook the turnips in salted boiling water until they are easily pierced with a knife, 7 to 10 minutes. The fresher the turnips are, the less cooking time they'll need. Drain and let them cool.

Remove the aluminum foil from the greens and cut each turnip into quarters. Butter a metal platter or shallow baking dish and arrange the turnip quarters on it. Season them with salt and pepper and put a small flake of the butter on each one.

FINISHING:

Heat the oven to 400°F. Slide the platter into the oven and let the turnips reheat for 5 minutes before serving.

This vegetable garnish is used in **Guinea Hen with New Turnips** (page 138).

desserts froids

COLD DESSERTS

APPLES IN RED WINE

TO SERVE 4:

1½ cups red wine
1 cup sugar
1 cinnamon stick
2 pounds (4 to 5) large apples
4 scoops **Vanilla Ice Cream** (page 203)

COOKING:

In a large shallow pan, cook the wine, sugar, and cinnamon for 10 minutes over medium-high heat. Peel the apples and cut balls from them with a melon baller. Put the apple balls in the warm wine. They shouldn't touch one another, which is why you need a large pan. Simmer the apples 5 to 7 minutes, partially covered. When they are cooked but still firm, remove them from the heat, cool, and refrigerate. The apple balls should macerate about 10 hours in the wine so that they take on a deep-red color.

PRESENTATION:

Serve the chilled apples as garnish for a scoop of vanilla ice cream per person.

APPLE SHERBET

FOR 1 QUART:

4 tart juicy apples
1 cup fresh unfiltered apple juice
1 cup sugar
½ lemon

Quarter and core the apples. Put them in a saucepan with the apple juice and sugar and cook over medium heat until soft, 5 to 10 minutes. Put this mixture in the food processor and purée. Squeeze the juice from the ½ lemon into the puréed apples and cool. Strain the mixture into an ice-cream churn or electric machine and freeze according to manufacturer's instructions.

*Bananes aux zestes
de citron vert et d'orange*

BANANAS WITH LIME AND ORANGE ZESTS

FOR 4 SERVINGS:

Scant ²/₃ cup sugar
½ orange
½ lime
4 bananas

PREPARATIONS:

Make a syrup by mixing the sugar with ²/₃ cup water in a small saucepan and bringing to a good boil. Remove the zest from the half orange and the half lime in strips and cut the zest strips into fine julienne. Squeeze the juice from the lime and the orange. Cut the bananas on the diagonal into ½-inch slices.

Mix the fruit juice, half of the zest, and all the bananas into the sugar syrup. Pour into a fruit bowl, sprinkle with the remaining zest, and let macerate for 3 hours in a cool place.

PRESENTATION:

Serve in the bowl, along with other fruit preparations such as **Berry Cocktail with Cassis** (page 194), **Kiwis with Passion Fruit Juice** (page 198), and **Oranges Marinated in Grand Marnier** (page 201).

BERRY COCKTAIL WITH CASSIS

FOR 4 SERVINGS:

½ pound green gooseberries (see **NOTE**)
½ pound red gooseberries (see **NOTE**)
½ pound black currants (see **NOTE**)
1 lemon
½ cup sugar
¼ cup cassis liqueur

PREPARATIONS:

Remove the stems from the berries if necessary. Cut the green gooseberries in half. Squeeze the juice from the lemon. Combine all the ingredients and let them macerate together for a few hours in the refrigerator.

PRESENTATION:

Serve in a fruit dish, along with other fruit preparations such as **Bananas with Lime and Orange Zests** (page 193), **Kiwis with Passion Fruit Juice** (page 198), and **Oranges Marinated in Grand Marnier** (page 201).

NOTE: *All the fruits are available in the United States, but you may have trouble getting them all at once. The recipe is flexible. You might use a pound of just one type of gooseberry, for instance. Red currants can be substituted for black ones. Their flavor is not so strong, but the combination is still excellent when they are substituted and perhaps even prettier. Ed.*

Glace au caramel
et glace caramel au pralin

CARAMEL ICE CREAM AND CARAMEL ICE CREAM WITH PRALINE

FOR 1 QUART:

2 vanilla beans
1 cup sugar
¾ cup heavy cream
8 egg yolks
1½ cups milk
⅓ cup chopped **praline** (page 246), for the Caramel Ice
    Cream with Praline

PREPARATIONS:

Split the vanilla beans lengthwise and then cut them into thirds crosswise. Put the vanilla and the sugar in a heavy pot over low heat. When the sugar starts to melt and brown, stir it with a wooden spoon or spatula until it reaches a very dark caramel color. Never increase the heat, that's the secret to success. When the sugar has turned to caramel, remove from the heat and add the cream. Be careful of splatters. Set the pot back over very low heat and stir with the spatula until the caramel liquefies completely and melts into the cream. Remove from the heat.

Whisk the egg yolks in a bowl. Put the milk in a pan and bring it to a boil. Slowly pour the boiling milk into the bowl with the yolks, whisking vigorously so that the yolks don't curdle. Whisk the yolk-and-milk mixture into the caramel cream and whisk over low heat until the custard thickens just enough to coat a spoon. Immediately pour it through a strainer into a bowl. Chill it.

Put the custard into an ice-cream churn or electric machine and freeze according to manufacturer's instructions.

TO MAKE CARAMEL ICE CREAM WITH PRALINE:

Just before churning in the ice-cream machine, add the praline to the chilled custard.

THREE CITRUS SHERBETS

FOR 1 ½ QUARTS EACH:

Sorbet au citron vert
LIME SHERBET

15 to 20 limes, to yield 2 cups juice
2 cups sugar

Sorbet à l'orange sanguine
BLOOD-ORANGE SHERBET

8 to 12 blood oranges, to yield 4 cups juice
1 ½ to 1 ¾ cups sugar

Sorbet au grape-fruit
GRAPEFRUIT SHERBET

4 to 6 grapefruits, to yield 4 cups juice
1 ½ cups sugar

PREPARATIONS:

Grate the zest from 1 of the limes into a bowl. Squeeze and measure each of the fruit juices. Put the lime juice into the bowl with the zest and the other juices into separate bowls. Add 2 cups of water to the lime juice and add the specified quantity of sugar to each juice. The quantity needed for blood oranges varies depending on their acidity. Stir to dissolve the sugar. Freeze each sherbet in turn in an ice-cream churn or electric machine according to manufacturer's instructions.

Sorbet au chocolat amer

BITTER CHOCOLATE SHERBET

FOR 1 QUART:

7 ounces unsweetened chocolate
1 ½ cups sugar
½ cup lukewarm water
1 ¾ ounces sweet chocolate

PREPARATIONS:

Melt the unsweetened chocolate slowly in a pan set in a water bath. When it is melted, mix in the sugar and the water. Grate the sweet chocolate into the mixture and let cool. Put in an ice-cream churn or electric machine and freeze according to manufacturer's instructions.

PRESENTATION:

The sherbet may be served with a few pieces of **Preserved Kumquats** (page 199).

Kiwis au jus
de fruits de la passion

KIWIS WITH PASSION FRUIT JUICE

FOR 4 TO 6 SERVINGS:

6 kiwis
⅓ cup passion fruit juice (see **NOTE**)
1 tablespoon sugar, or to taste

PREPARATIONS:

Peel the kiwis, slice them, and arrange in a shallow dish. In a small saucepan, heat the passion fruit juice and sugar to taste and bring almost to a boil. Pour the warm juice over the kiwi slices and let macerate 3 hours in a cool place.

PRESENTATION:

Serve with other fruit preparations such as **Bananas with Lime and Orange Zests** (page 193), **Berry Cocktail with Cassis** (page 194), and **Oranges Marinated in Grand Marnier** (page 201).

NOTE: *Unsweetened passion fruit juice is available in health food stores. Ed.*

PRESERVED KUMQUATS

TO SERVE 4:

1 ½ pounds kumquats
2 cups water
1 ¼ cups sugar

COOKING:

Cut the kumquats into quarters and put them in a saucepan with the water and the sugar. Cook over low heat for 30 minutes. Pour the kumquats into a bowl and chill.

PRESENTATION:

Serve alone, or with other fruit preparations, or with **Bitter Chocolate Sherbet** (page 197).

MELON SHERBET

TO MAKE A GENEROUS PINT:

1 ripe melon, about 2½ pounds to yield 1 pound flesh
1 lemon
¾ cup sugar, approximately

PREPARATIONS:

Peel and seed the melon and weigh out 1 pound of the flesh. Cut it into chunks. Whir the melon, the juice of the lemon, and the sugar in a food processor to make a smooth mixture. Taste and add 2 to 3 tablespoons more sugar if you like. Put through a fine strainer, pour into an ice-cream churn or electric machine, and freeze according to manufacturer's instructions.

ORANGES MARINATED IN GRAND MARNIER

TO SERVE 4:

6 oranges
½ cup sugar
2 tablespoons Grand Marnier, plus a few drops
1 tablespoon grenadine

PREPARATIONS:

Remove the zest in wide bands from 1½ oranges. Cut the bands into very thin julienne strips. Blanch the zest 1 minute in boiling water, rinse under cold water, drain, and set aside. With a knife, peel all the oranges completely down to the flesh, removing the peeling in vertical bands. Working over a bowl so that you catch the juice, cut out the sections from the membranes. Squeeze the membranes to get all the juice.

COOKING:

Put the sugar in a large saucepan and cook over medium heat until the sugar begins to brown. Add the reserved orange juice and continue cooking until you have a light syrup. Remove any scum. Add the orange zest, the Grand Marnier, and the grenadine and bring to a boil. Add the orange sections and shake well so that they are completely covered with the syrup. Leave on the burner just long enough to get them hot but not to cook them. Remove from the heat and chill. To strengthen the flavor, add a few drops of Grand Marnier to the oranges after removing them from the heat.

PRESENTATION:

Serve the oranges on plates, each serving arranged in a star shape and napped with the sauce. Or serve in a compote, along with a selection of other prepared fruits such as **Bananas with Lime and Orange Zests** (page 193), **Berry Cocktail with Cassis** (page 194), and **Kiwis with Passion Fruit Juice** (page 198).

WILD STRAWBERRY MOUSSE

TO SERVE 4:

10 ounces wild strawberries (see **NOTE**)
½ cup sugar
¼ lemon
10 tablespoons champagne
Powdered sugar

PREPARATIONS:

Put ⅓ cup of the strawberries in a small bowl, add ½ teaspoon of the sugar, and squeeze a few drops of lemon juice over them. Mix gently and set aside to macerate. Purée the remaining strawberries with the rest of the sugar and 6 tablespoons of the champagne in a food processor. Squeeze ½ teaspoon lemon juice into the purée and stir.

FINISHING AND PRESENTATION:

Frost 4 stemmed glasses by moistening the rims with lemon juice and then dipping them in powdered sugar. Put one quarter of the macerated strawberries in each of the glasses and pour 1 tablespoon champagne over each. Fill with the strawberry mousse. Put them in the freezer for 30 minutes before serving to chill well.

NOTE: *Once found only in the wild, tiny fraises des bois are now cultivated and widely available in Europe. They are not so easy to find in the United States. When regular strawberries are at their best, they will make a good mousse. Put halved or quartered berries in the bottoms of the glasses.*

Glace à la vanille

VANILLA ICE CREAM

FOR 1½ QUARTS:

2 vanilla beans
1 ¼ cups sugar
6 egg yolks
1 ¾ cups milk
2 cups heavy cream

PREPARATIONS:

Split the vanilla beans and scrape the grains into a bowl. Save the emptied beans. Sprinkle 1 tablespoon of the sugar over the vanilla grains and mix thoroughly to separate all the grains so that they will be distributed through the ice cream rather than cling together in bunches. Add the remaining sugar and the egg yolks and whisk until the mixture lightens in color.

Put the milk in a saucepan, add the emptied vanilla beans, and bring to a boil. Remove the vanilla beans. Pour the boiling milk into the egg and sugar mixture, whisking vigorously. Return the entire mixture to the pan and thicken it over low heat, stirring constantly with a wooden spatula, until it thickens enough to coat the spatula. Add the cream, strain into a bowl, and chill.

Pour into an ice-cream churn or electric machine and freeze according to manufacturer's instructions.

desserts chauds

WARM DESSERTS

CHERRY SOUFFLÉ

TO SERVE 4:

1 to 1½ pounds cherries (14 ounces pitted weight)
2 tablespoons butter
10 tablespoons sugar
2 tablespoons kirsch
1 lemon
1 egg yolk
2 egg whites

PREPARATIONS:

Pit the cherries. Melt the butter in a frying pan over medium-high heat. Brown the cherries in the butter and add 5 tablespoons of the sugar. Continue cooking until the sugar carmelizes lightly. Add the kirsch to the pan, flame, and remove from the heat. Put the cherries in a strainer to drain them and reserve both the cherries and the cooking liquid. (The cherries can be cooked the day before serving the soufflé.)

FINISHING AND PRESENTATION:

Heat the oven to 500 °F. Squeeze 1½ tablespoons lemon juice. Put the cherries in four small soufflé dishes about 3 inches in diameter. Add enough of the juice to just cover the cherries. If the juice has reduced too much, add a little water so that you have enough.

In a bowl, whisk the egg yolk and 2½ tablespoons of the sugar until it lightens in color; add ½ tablespoon of the lemon juice. In another bowl, beat the egg whites and 1 tablespoon sugar to soft peaks. Add the remaining 1½ tablespoons sugar, beat until the whites are very firm, and then fold in the remaining tablespoon lemon juice. Stir one third of the beaten egg whites into the yolks and then fold in the rest of the whites, mixing gently.

Fill the soufflé dishes with the soufflé mixture. Put the soufflés on the floor of the preheated oven for 5 minutes. Remove and serve immediately.

CRÊPES ALASKA

TO SERVE 4:

Crêpe batter:

2 whole eggs
1 cup less 2 tablespoons milk
2 tablespoons melted butter or oil
1 pinch salt
1 cup flour
3 tablespoons sugar

Sauce:

2 oranges
3 lemons
⅔ cup sugar

2 teaspoons butter
½ pint **Vanilla Ice Cream** (page 203)
Powdered sugar, for sprinkling

PREPARATIONS:

For the crêpe batter, simply mix together all the ingredients listed. If the batter is lumpy, strain it. It does not need to rest before being used.

Remove the zest in strips from half an orange and then cut the strips crosswise into very fine julienne. Squeeze ¾ cup orange juice and ⅓ cup lemon juice. Put the juices in a saucepan with the ⅔ cup sugar and the julienned orange zest and reduce over high heat to ¾ cup of syrupy liquid; this will take about 5 minutes. Remove from the heat and set aside.

COOKING AND PRESENTATION:

Prepare 8 thin crêpes using two small non-stick frying pans. Melt the 2 teaspoons butter and brush a little bit of it on the first pan. Put about 2 tablespoons of the crêpe batter in the pan. Turn and tilt the pan so the batter covers the bottom of the skillet and then put it on a burner over high heat. Turn the crêpe when it starts to swell in the center and brown around the edge and if needed add a little more butter. Cook for a few seconds on the second side until it is speckled brown. Remove the crêpe and set aside.

Repeat with a second crêpe, this time using the other pan so that the first has a chance to cool. If the first pan does not cool off enough before you start on the third crêpe, run cold water over the outside of it for several seconds. It's important that the pan cool; otherwise the batter will stick to the hot pan when it is put in and will be irregularly shaped and thicker in some spots than others. Continue making the crêpes, alternating between pans until you have prepared all eight. Brush the pans with more butter if the crêpes stick and pile the crêpes on top of each other as they're made in order to keep them warm.

Heat the broiler. Reheat the sauce. Working quickly, put a spoonful of vanilla ice cream in each warm crêpe and then fold in half like a turnover. Put two folded crêpes on each of four plates, sprinkle with powdered sugar, and put them under the broiler for 30 seconds. Nap the crêpes with the warm sauce and serve immediately.

Gratin d'oranges
"Madame France"

ORANGE GRATIN

TO SERVE 4:

16 orange segments prepared according to the recipe for
Oranges Marinated in Grand Marnier (page 201;
about ⅓ of the recipe) and ¼ cup of their liquid
¼ cup **pastry cream** (page 245)
1½ tablespoons orange marmalade
10 tablespoons heavy cream
A few drops Grand Marnier or other orange-flavored brandy
1 teaspoon chopped pistachios

PREPARATIONS:

Prepare the oranges and the pastry cream. Whisk together the pastry cream, the marmalade, the orange liquid from the oranges, and ¼ cup of the heavy cream. Stir well to combine thoroughly. Add the Grand Marnier. Whip the remaining 6 tablespoons cream and mix it into the pastry cream mixture.

Arrange the orange segments in a small gratin dish about 5 to 6 inches in diameter and pour the orange cream mixture over them.

FINISHING:

Heat the broiler. Put the oranges under the broiler a few moments to brown the surface of the cream. Sprinkle with the chopped pistachios and serve immediately.

Petit soufflé d'agrumes aux kiwis

ORANGE SOUFFLÉ WITH KIWI

TO SERVE 4:

4 oranges
½ lime
1 cup sugar
2 kiwis
Butter for the molds
2 egg yolks
4 egg whites

PREPARATIONS:

Remove the zest in strips from half an orange and cut the strips crosswise into very fine julienne. Squeeze the juice from two of the oranges and the half lime and put the juices into a saucepan with the orange zest and ⅓ cup of the sugar. Bring to a boil and continue boiling over high heat for 5 to 6 minutes until syrupy. Remove from the heat and set aside.

Peel the kiwis and cut each of them into 12 sections, slicing from the top to the bottom of the fruit. Keep 16 of these sections for the garnish and cut up the remaining 8 sections. Set all the kiwi aside in a bowl, covered to protect it from the air.

With a knife, cut the skin from the remaining 2 oranges, including all the white pith.

Do this over a bowl to catch all the juice. Cut out the sections from between the membranes and squeeze the juice from any pulp remaining attached to the membrane.

Use a pastry brush to butter the insides and rims of four small soufflé molds about 2 inches in diameter.

FINISHING:

Heat the oven to 525°F. In a bowl, whisk the egg yolks and ⅓ cup of the sugar until the yolks lighten in color and are quite frothy. In another bowl, beat together the egg whites with half the remaining ⅓ cup sugar to soft peaks. Add the rest of the sugar and beat until the whites are stiff.

Fill a flameproof baking dish about one third full with water. Put the dish over medium heat so that when the soufflés are ready to cook the water bath will be heated just to the edge of boiling. Fold 1 tablespoon of the orange juice from the reserved orange sections into the beaten egg whites and then stir one third of the whites into the yolk mixture. Add the rest of the whites and fold in carefully.

Fill the molds with the soufflé mixture and put them in the water bath. Cook them on top of the stove, with the water simmering, for 3 minutes. Remove the soufflé dishes from the water bath, put them on the floor of the preheated oven, and let them finish cooking for 3 minutes. Meanwhile, reheat the orange sauce and add the chopped kiwi to it.

PRESENTATION:

Unmold the soufflés onto warm plates. Decorate each plate with 4 sections of kiwi and six orange sections. Nap with the orange sauce and serve immediately.

Soufflé au fruit de la passion

PASSION FRUIT SOUFFLÉ

TO SERVE 2:

1 egg yolk
6 tablespoons sugar
2 egg whites
½ cup passion fruit juice (see **NOTE** page 198)
Buttter for the mold

COOKING:

Heat the oven to 400°F. In a bowl, whisk the egg yolk and 2 ½ tablespoons of the sugar until the mixture lightens in color. In another bowl, beat the egg whites and 1 tablespoon of the sugar to soft peaks and then add 1 ½ tablespoons sugar and beat to firm peaks. Mix 2 tablespoons passion fruit juice into the yolk mixture and then stir in one third of the egg white mixture. When this is incorporated, add the rest of the egg whites, folding them in with a spatula.

Use a pastry brush to butter a 5-inch soufflé mold and then fill the mold with the soufflé mixture. Put the soufflé in the preheated oven for about 10 to 12 minutes. While the soufflé is cooking, add the remaining 1 tablespoon of sugar to the rest of the passion fruit juice and heat very gently so that the sugar dissolves and the juice is just lukewarm.

PRESENTATION:

Take the soufflé to the table in its dish with the sauce in a small sauceboat. Divide the soufflé between two plates and pour sauce over each portion.

pâtisserie

PASTRY

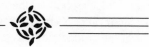

ALMOND RASPBERRY CAKE

TO SERVE 6:

⅓ cup raspberries
9 tablespoons sugar
1 lemon
2⅔ ounces (about ¾ cup) ground almonds
2 egg whites
3½ ounces **puff pastry** (page 241; see **NOTE**)
¼ cup sliced almonds
1 tablespoon powdered sugar

PREPARATIONS:

Whir the raspberries and 3 tablespoons of the granulated sugar in a food processor and then, if you don't like biting on raspberry seeds, strain the purée. Grate the zest from the lemon into a bowl. Add the ground almonds, the remaining 6 tablespoons granulated sugar, and the egg whites and stir to combine.

Roll out the puff pastry to a thin round ¹⁄₁₆ to ⅛ inch thick. Line a 7-inch tart pan with the pastry and prick the bottom thoroughly with a fork. If you are not going to cook the pastry right away, refrigerate it.

COOKING:

Heat the oven to 425°F. Sprinkle the powdered sugar over the pastry and then spread the raspberry purée over the pastry in a smooth layer. Put the almond mixture on top of the purée and use a spatula to smooth the surface. Bake for 20 minutes in a preheated oven and then reduce the temperature to 350°F and cook for 20 minutes longer. Remove the cake from the oven and let it cool to lukewarm. Heat the broiler.

Sprinkle the sliced almonds over the surface of the cake and dust with the powdered sugar. Put the cake under the broiler to brown the almonds and lightly caramelize the sugar. Watch it carefully; this should not take more than 1 or 2 minutes. Cool thoroughly before unmolding.

NOTE: *Since the puff pastry in this recipe should not rise, you can use scraps left from another recipe. Ed.*

BLACK FOREST CAKE

TO SERVE 6:

Chocolate sponge cake (page 244)
1 cup sweetened canned pitted cherries
2 tablespons kirsch
6 ounces semisweet chocolate
¼ cup granulated sugar
1 ¼ cups heavy cream
1 tablespoon powdered sugar

PREPARATIONS:

The day before serving, prepare the chocolate sponge cake. At least 3 hours before you begin to assemble the cake, cut the cherries in halves, put them in a bowl, and add the kirsch. Heat the chocolate in a water bath over low heat until it is just melted. Meanwhile, chill a large baking sheet without sides under cold water and then dry it. Using a spatula, spread the melted chocolate on the baking sheet in a thin, even layer. Let it harden in the refrigerator or in a cool place.

Put 2 tablespoons of the sugar and 3 tablespoons water in a small pan and heat to melt the sugar. Add a few drops of the kirsch from the cherries. Use a serrated knife to cut the cake into three layers horizontally. Place them on a work surface and use a pastry brush to brush the top of each with the syrup. Sprinkle a few drops of the kirsch on the surface of each of the cake layers. Whip the cream together with the remaining 2 tablespoons of sugar and a teaspoon of the kirsch.

FINISHING:

Drain the cherries. Spread one third of the whipped cream on the first layer of the cake and then arrange half the cherries on the cream. Place a second layer of cake on top of the first and then cover it, as you did the first, with a layer of one third of the cream and half the cherries. Place the third layer of cake on top of the other two. Mask the sides of the cake with the rest of the whipped cream.

Using a long metal spatula, start at one end of the baking sheet of chilled chocolate and, with the blade of the spatula grasped between thumb and forefinger, push up to the other end making a curled band of chocolate. Scrape all the chocolate into curls in this way. Garnish the top of the cake with chocolate curls, sprinkle with the powdered sugar, and refrigerate until ready to serve.

Tarte vaudoise à la crème

CREAM TART VAUDOISE STYLE

TO SERVE 8:

Pastry:

1 cup flour
1 ½ teaspoons baking powder
4 tablespoons butter, softened
1 pinch salt
¼ teaspoon sugar
3 to 4 tablespoons milk

Filling:

1 cup heavy cream
½ cup sugar
½ teaspoon flour
⅛ teaspoon powdered cinnamon

PREPARATIONS:

Heat the oven to 350°F. Put the 1 cup flour, the baking powder, butter, salt, and ¼ teaspoon sugar in a bowl. Work the mixture with your fingertips until it has the consistency of meal. Stir in the milk, form the dough into a ball, and roll it in any loose flour remaining on the bottom of the bowl. If the flour is not readily absorbed, add a few drops of milk.

Without letting the dough rest, roll it out in a thin round about ⅛ inch thick. Butter and then lightly flour a 10-inch tart pan with a removable base. Line the pan loosely with the dough leaving about ⅓ inch of slack. Carefully press the slack down the edge and into the center of the pan so that the pastry is level with the rim of the pan and then "fix" it at the base of the side by pressing with your thumbs. If any of the slack is still beyond the rim, cut it off.

To make the border that we use for all of our tarts at Crissier, first push the dough around the side back up above the rim. Fold the dough back and press with your fingers making a rolled edge even with the top of the rim. Now pinch the edge between your thumb and index finger every ⅓ inch or so all along the rim. Prick the base of the dough thoroughly with a fork.

Bake the pastry shell in the preheated oven until nut brown and almost fully cooked, about 20 minutes. Remove and let cool. Put the cream for the filling in a small saucepan and reduce over medium heat to ¾ cup, about 10 minutes. Set aside to cool.

COOKING:

Heat the oven to 375°F. Mix the sugar for the filling with the flour and then spread this mixture over the bottom of the pastry, shaking the pan so that the mixture covers the dough evenly. Pour the cream into the tart pan and use your fingertips to mix it with the sugar so that the filling is evenly distributed over the pastry in a thin layer. Powder with the cinnamon, put a few flecks of butter on the surface and set the tart in the preheated oven to bake for 20 minutes. Cool to lukewarm and unmold. (**NOTE:** *Remove the rim of the pan and remove the tart from the pan base to a rack, using two long spatulas which you slide in an X between the crust and the pan bottom. Ed.*) Let the tart cool completely.

Galettes au miel

HONEY CAKES

TO SERVE 6 TO 8:

½ pound **sweet pastry** (page 242)
2 tablespoons apricot preserves
⅔ cup sugar
1½ cups sliced almonds
6 tablespoons butter
2 tablespoons honey
2 tablespoons cream
⅓ cup chopped candied fruit
1 teaspoon kirsch

PREPARATIONS:

Prepare the sweet pastry and chill. Heat the oven to 400°F.

Roll the pastry out into a round ⅛ inch thick. Line a 9-inch tart pan with a removable base with the pastry and then prick the bottom thoroughly with a fork. Bake the tart shell on the floor of the preheated oven until browned, 8 to 10 minutes. Melt the apricot preserves over low heat and strain.

COOKING:

Heat the oven to 400°F. Use a pastry brush to paint a thin glaze of the strained apricot preserves on the bottom of the pastry shell. Put all the remaining ingredients in a saucepan and cook over low heat, stirring, until the mixture is smooth and has melted together, and spread it in the tart shell. Cook in the preheated oven until the filling starts to bubble, 10 to 15 minutes. Remove from the oven and set it aside to cool.

PRESENTATION:

Remove from the mold, cut into small triangular or rectangular cakes, and serve with coffee.

COMMENT: These petits fours are very practical because they keep well.

Tarte au citron

LEMON TART

TO SERVE 6:

½ pound **sweet pastry** (page 242)
1 orange
3 lemons
3 whole eggs
1 egg yolk
⅔ cup heavy cream
¾ cup sugar

PREPARATIONS:

Prepare the sweet pastry and chill. Heat the oven to 400°F. Squeeze the juice from the orange and lemons.

Butter an 8-inch tart pan with a removable base and flour it lightly. Roll out the pastry to a round about ⅛ inch thick and line the tart pan loosely with the dough leaving about ⅓ inch of slack. Carefully press the slack down the edge and into the center of the pan so that the pastry is level with the top of the pan and then "fix" it at the base of the side by pressing with your thumbs. If any of the slack is still beyond the rim, cut it off.

To make the border, first push the dough around the side back up above the rim. Fold the dough back and press with your fingers making a rolled edge even with the top of the rim. Now pinch the edge between your thumb and index finger every ⅓ inch or so all along the rim. Prick the base of the dough thoroughly with a fork. Press a piece of aluminum foil over the pastry. Cook the shell, without browning, in the preheated oven for 15 minutes. Remove and let cool.

COOKING:

Heat the oven to 350°F. Whisk together all the ingredients for the lemon filling: the whole eggs, the yolk, the fruit juice, the cream, and the sugar. When the mixture is foamy, pour most of it into the tart shell and put the tart in the preheated oven. Once the tart is in the oven, fill the shell with the remaining filling, using a spoon to spread it out to the edge. The tart shell should now be so full it cannot be moved without spilling.

Let the tart cook with the oven door ajar until the filling sets, 30 to 35 minutes. Check for doneness by lightly shaking the tart shell. The filling should be thickened but still quite wobbly. It will firm as it cools. Remove the tart from the pan when it has cooled to lukewarm and set it on a rack to cool completely (see **NOTE** page 217).

RAISINÉ TART

TO SERVE 6:

½ pound **sweet pastry** (page 242)
3 whole eggs
1 egg yolk
½ cup heavy cream
⅓ cup raisiné (see **COMMENT** and **NOTE**)

PREPARATIONS:

Prepare the sweet pastry and chill. Heat the oven to 400°F.

Lightly butter and flour an 8-inch tart pan with a removable base. Roll the dough out to a round ⅛ inch thick. Line the pan loosely with the dough leaving about ⅓ inch of slack. Carefully press the slack back toward the center of the pan so that the pastry is level with the rim. Use your thumbs to press the dough at the base of the side against the pan to "fix" it there. Cut off any pastry that remains beyond the rim.

To make the border, first push the dough around the side of the pan back up above the edge of the rim. Fold this over to make a rolled edge even with the top of the rim. Now pinch the edge of the pastry every ⅓ inch between your thumb and index finger to make a decorative border.

Prick the bottom of the pastry with a fork. Press a piece of aluminum foil over the pastry. Cook the pastry without letting it brown in the preheated oven for 15 minutes. Remove and let cool.

COOKING:

Heat the oven to 350°F. Prepare the tart filling by whisking together the eggs, egg yolk, cream, and raisiné. Pour part of this mixture into the tart shell and then set the tart in the preheated oven. Once the tart is in the oven, finish filling it to the brim. Bake the tart in the preheated oven about 30 minutes with the door ajar. Check for doneness by lightly shaking the pan. Remove when still wobbly but no longer liquid. Unmold the tart after it's cooled a bit but is still lukewarm and let it finish cooling on a rack (see **NOTE** page 217).

COMMENT: This is an old recipe of the Vaudois region. All over the countryside, cooks slowly reduce apple and pear juice to make the raisiné.

NOTE: *To make a substitute for the raisiné, put 1 cup fresh unfiltered apple or pear juice, a small piece of orange zest, and a few specks of ground cinnamon and clove in a small saucepan and reduce over low heat to ⅓ cup. Ed.*

Tarte aux framboises

RASPBERRY TART

TO SERVE 4:

½ pound **sweet pastry** (page 242)
1 whole egg
2 egg yolks
⅓ cup sugar
⅓ cup heavy cream
½ pound raspberries

PREPARATIONS:

Prepare the sweet pastry and chill. Heat the oven to 400°F.

Butter and flour a 7- to 8-inch tart pan with a removable base. Roll the pastry out into a round ⅛ inch thick. Line the pan loosely with the dough leaving about ⅓ inch of slack. Carefully press the slack into the center of the pan so that it is about level with the rim of the pan and then use your thumbs to "fix" it all around the base of the side. If any of the slack is still beyond the rim, cut it off.

To make a border, first push the dough back up the side to extend above the rim. Fold this dough back and press with your fingers to make a rolled edge even with the rim. Now pinch the edge between your thumb and index finger every ⅓ inch or so.

With a fork, prick the base of the dough. Press a sheet of aluminum foil over the pastry. Cook the tart shell, without browning it, in the preheated oven for 15 minutes. Remove and let cool.

In a bowl, whisk together the whole egg, egg yolks, sugar, and cream. Arrange the raspberries, stem end down, in the cooked tart shell in concentric circles.

Heat the oven to 375°F. Cover the raspberries with the tart filling and bake the tart in the preheated oven for 40 minutes. Check occasionally to be sure that the filling does not boil during cooking. Cool the tart thoroughly before unmolding (see **NOTE** page 217).

Génoise aux fraises des bois

WILD STRAWBERRY CAKE

TO SERVE 6:

Sponge cake (page 243)
5 tablespoons sugar
¼ teaspoon framboise or fraises des bois eau-de-vie
2 tablespoons sliced almonds
1⅔ cups heavy cream
¾ pound wild strawberries (see **NOTE** page 202)
Royal icing (page 247)

PREPARATIONS:

The day before serving, make the sponge cake. The next day, put 2 tablespoons of the sugar and 3 tablespoons water in a small pan and heat to melt the sugar. Add a few drops of eau-de-vie. Toast the almonds in a 350°F oven about 15 minutes. Stir them occasionally so that they color evenly.

Use a serrated knife to cut the cake horizontally into three layers. Lay the layers on a work surface and brush them lightly with the sugar syrup. Whip the cream together with the remaining 3 tablespoons sugar.

FINISHING:

Set aside about ½ cup whipped cream. Spread half the remaining whipped cream on the bottom layer of cake and arrange one third of the strawberries on the cream. Put the second cake layer on top of this, cover it with the rest of the whipped cream (except the reserved ½ cup), and add another third of the strawberries. Now place the final layer on top, press the top of the cake lightly to even it, and use a spatula to smooth the cream that has escaped from between the layers around the edges of the cake. Set aside while you prepare the royal icing.

Pour the icing on the top of the cake and let it spread itself out for a few moments. Then use a spatula heated under hot water to spread the icing evenly. Spread carefully so as not to get any crumbs in the icing and heat the spatula two or three times as necessary. Garnish the top with the remaining strawberries. Pipe the reserved whipped cream around the top edge, and stick the almonds into the cream. Refrigerate until serving. This cake should be served the same day that it is made.

Mille-feuille aux fraises

STRAWBERRY NAPOLEON

TO SERVE 6:

¼ pound strawberries (see **COMMENT**)
½ pound **puff pastry** (page 241)
1 egg yolk
1 tablespoon water
1 tablespoon powdered sugar
¾ cup heavy cream
⅓ cup granulated sugar
2 tablespoons **pastry cream** (page 245)
1 tablespoon framboise eau-de-vie (see **COMMENT**)

PREPARATIONS:

Heat the oven to 425°F. Hull the strawberries and cut them into ½-inch dice. Roll out the puff pastry to a square 12 inches on each side and about ⅛ inch thick. Put it on a baking sheet and prick thoroughly with a fork, every ½ inch or so.

Mix the egg yolk with the water to make a glaze and then with a pastry brush paint the surface of the puff pastry with the glaze. Put the puff pastry in the preheated oven and cook for 10 minutes. Reduce heat to 375°F and cook 15 to 20 minutes longer. Check it occasionally but remember that the success of good puff pastry depends upon its being well cooked and very dry. When the pastry is done, remove the sheet from the oven and sprinkle some of the powdered sugar on the pastry. Put it under the broiler for a few seconds to caramelize the sugar. Remove and let cool.

When the pastry is cool, trim the edges so that they are even and cut the pastry into three equal bands. Turn the bands over, sprinkle them with some powdered sugar and put them under the broiler again for a few seconds to caramelize the sugar. Remove and let cool again.

FINISHING:

Whip the cream, add the granulated sugar, the pastry cream, and the framboise, and whisk together. Put one of the bands of puff pastry on a serving platter. Spread a ½-inch-thick layer of cream filling on the pastry and then put half the strawberry dice in the layer of cream and cover them with additional cream. Put the second band of puff pastry on top of this and cover it with cream, strawberries, and more cream exactly as before. Place the final band of puff pastry on top. Coat the sides evenly with the remaining cream.

COMMENT: In winter we replace the strawberries with pineapple and the framboise with kirsch.

Biscuit pour
le thé de Fanny

TEA CAKE

TO SERVE 8:

¾ cup sugar
3 whole eggs
1 pinch salt
1 lemon
6 tablespoons butter, softened, plus butter for the loaf pan
1⅔ cups all-purpose flour
⅔ cup cake flour
⅔ cup milk
⅓ cup heavy cream
1 tablespoon baking powder

COOKING:

Heat the oven to 350°F. In the large bowl, whisk together the sugar, eggs, and salt until frothy. Grate the zest from the lemon over this mixture. Add the butter and the flour and mix briskly with a spatula or wooden spoon until the batter is very smooth. Add the milk, the cream, and the baking powder and work them in thoroughly with the spatula.

Butter a loaf pan about 12 by 4 inches. Put the batter in the pan and tap the pan on a hard surface to level the batter. Cook the cake in the preheated oven about 1 hour, or until it tests done.

COMMENT: The cake is best made the day before serving.

Tarte au vin

WINE TART

TO SERVE 6:

Pastry:

1 cup flour
4 tablespoons butter, softened
1 ½ teaspoons baking powder
1 pinch salt
¼ teaspoon sugar
3 to 4 tablespoons milk

Filling:

⅔ cup sugar
1 teaspoon powdered cinnamon
1 ½ tablespoons flour
⅓ cup white wine
1 tablespoon butter

PREPARATIONS:

To make the pastry, in a bowl, work together the 1 cup flour, 4 tablespoons butter, the baking powder, salt, and ¼ teaspoon sugar with your fingertips until the mixture has the consistency of meal. Stir in the milk, form the dough into a ball, and roll the ball in any loose flour remaining on the bottom of the bowl. If the flour is not readily absorbed, add a few drops of milk.

Butter and flour an 8-inch tart pan with a removable base. Without letting the dough rest, roll it out to a round about ⅓ inch thick. Line the pan loosely with the dough leaving about ⅓ inch of slack. Carefully press the slack back into the center of the pan so that it is nearly level with the rim and then use your thumbs to press the dough around the base of the side of the pan to "fix" it there. Cut off any of the slack that remains beyond the rim.

To make the border, first push the dough back up above the rim. Fold the dough back and press with your fingers to make a rolled edge even with the top of the rim. Pinch the edge between your thumb and index finger every ⅓ inch all along the rim. Prick the base of the tart shell.

COOKING:

Heat the oven to 375°F. Mix together the ⅔ cup sugar, the cinnamon, and the 1½ tablespoons flour. Sprinkle the mixture in the pastry shell, spreading evenly. Add the wine and, with your fingertips, incorporate it into the flour mixture. Dot with the 1 tablespoon butter.

Bake the tart on the floor of the preheated oven for 20 minutes. Turn the pan occasionally to equalize the cooking and to avoid the formation of bubbles in the filling. Let the tart cool before unmolding.

préparations de base

BASIC RECIPES

VEGETABLE BOUILLON

FOR 1 QUART:

1 leek
1 large carrot
½ small celery root
1 large onion
2 shallots
6 garlic cloves
½ teaspoon peppercorns
1 quart white wine
1 quart water
2 tomatoes
1 bouquet garni
1 teaspoon salt

COOKING:

Chop the leek, carrot, celery root, onion, and shallots. Cut the garlic cloves in half. Crush the peppercorns. Put all the ingredients listed in a large pot. Bring to a boil, reduce the heat, and simmer, partially covered, 3 hours, stirring occasionally. Strain.

COMMENT: Because the taste is more subtle, I often use this instead of fish stock, especially for butter sauces.

Fond de poisson

FISH STOCK

FOR 2 CUPS:

1 leek
2 pounds bones, heads, and tails from sole, turbot, or other lean
    white fish
2 cups white wine
2 cups water
1 carrot
1 rib celery
1 onion, stuck with a clove
2 sprigs parsley
1 bay leaf

COOKING:

Cut off and discard the leek greens and wash the leek. Rinse the fish bones under cold
running water, break them into large pieces, and put them in a saucepan. Add the white
wine and the water. Bring to a boil, over low heat, skimming often. Add the leek, carrot,
celery, onion, parsley, and bay leaf and cook, uncovered and still over low heat, for 30
minutes. Strain the stock and, if necessary, reduce it over high heat to 2 cups.

Fond d'écrevisses

CRAYFISH STOCK

FOR ¾ CUP:

2 carrots
2 onions
2 garlic cloves
32 crayfish shells
2 tablespoons olive oil
2 to 3 cups white wine
4 sprigs parsley
2 sprigs thyme
2 sprigs rosemary

PREPARATIONS:

Chop the carrots, onions, and garlic. Crush the crayfish shells in a food processor in three batches. It's all right if there are still some chunks of shell. Heat the olive oil in a saucepan over high heat. Add the crayfish shells and the chopped vegetables and brown, stirring. Reduce the heat to medium and continue cooking until all the water released by the shells and vegetables evaporates. Add white wine to barely cover the vegetables and then put in the parsley, thyme, and rosemary. Cook gently over low heat, uncovered, for 1 hour. Stir occasionally and add water if the liquid evaporates to less than ¾ cup. Strain the stock.

Beurre d'écrevisses

CRAYFISH BUTTER

FOR ABOUT ⅜ CUP:

1 head garlic
1 onion
½ rib celery
1 tablespoon olive oil
32 crayfish carcasses (see **COMMENT**)
6 tablespoons butter, softened
⅓ cup white wine
2 to 3 cups water
3 sprigs parsley
2 sprigs thyme
1 sprig rosemary

COOKING:

Cut the garlic and the onion in half horizontally and chop the celery. Brown them in the olive oil over medium-high heat and set aside. Put the crayfish carcasses and the butter in the food processor in three batches, whirring each batch until the shells are crushed. It's all right if there are still some chunks of shell. Add the butter and crushed shells to the garlic, onion, and celery. Brown over medium-high heat, stirring occasionally until a light, crusty layer forms on the bottom of the pan. Now add the wine and enough water to barely cover the crayfish. Add the parsley, thyme, and rosemary, reduce the heat to low, and cook for 30 minutes.

Strain the cooked mixture through a fine sieve and press the shells and vegetables firmly with a spoon to squeeze all the juices through. Refrigerate so that the butter rises to the surface. Scrape the solidified crayfish butter from the top and store it in the refrigerator.

COMMENT: Four lobster carcasses or 12 lobsterette carcasses are substituted for the crayfish, depending on the recipe being made.

Fond de volaille

CHICKEN STOCK

FOR 2½ QUARTS:

1 leek
1 rib celery
2 carrots
1 garlic clove
One 5- to 6-pound stewing hen, with giblets
About 4½ quarts water
1 onion, stuck with a clove
1 bouquet garni

COOKING:

Cut off and discard the green leaves from the leek and wash the rest of it. Chop the leek, the celery, and carrots. Crush the garlic clove. Put the chicken and the giblets in a pot of cold unsalted water, bring to a boil, and add all the vegetables and the bouquet garni. Turn the heat down and simmer, uncovered, for 4 hours, skimming often.

Carefully remove the chicken from the pot. The meat can be used for making chicken croquettes and the like. Strain the stock, chill it, and remove the fat.

Fond blanc

WHITE STOCK

FOR ABOUT 1½ QUARTS:

1 veal knuckle, chopped into pieces
½ calf's foot, chopped into pieces
2 chicken carcasses, broken up
1 teaspoon peppercorns
1 leek
½ small celery root
2 onions, each stuck with a clove
2 carrots
1 bouquet garni

COOKING:

Put the veal knuckle, the calf's foot, and the chicken carcasses in a large pot of cold water, bring to a boil, and blanch at a low boil for 5 minutes. Drain. Crush the peppercorns. Cut off and discard the green top from the leek and wash the rest. Peel the celery root.

Put the bones in a large stockpot, cover with water, and slowly bring to a boil, skimming often. When the liquid reaches a full boil, add the vegetables, the bouquet garni, and the crushed peppercorns and cook over low heat for 4 hours, uncovered, skimming from time to time. Strain the stock, put it back in the pot, and reduce it over high heat until it has the consistency of an aspic. To test whether or not it has reduced enough, pour a thin layer onto a plate and put it in the freezer. It should set in 2 minutes.

Fond de veau et glace de veau

VEAL STOCK AND VEAL GLAZE

FOR 1½ QUARTS STOCK OR 2 CUPS GLAZE:

2 pounds veal bones, chopped into pieces
2 carrots
1 onion
1 leek
1 shallot
1 bouquet garni
1 garlic clove

COOKING:

Heat the oven to 400°F. Put the veal bones in a roasting pan and cook in the oven until they brown, about 30 minutes. Chop the carrots, onion, leek, and shallot. Put the browned bones, the vegetables, the bouquet garni, and the garlic in a stockpot. Add enough water to completely cover the bones and slowly bring the liquid to a boil, skimming to remove fat and scum. Reduce the heat to low and continue to cook, uncovered, for 4 hours, skimming occasionally and adding water whenever necessary to keep the veal bones covered. Strain the stock.

VEAL GLAZE:

Proceed as above and then reduce the strained stock by two thirds so that each cup of stock yields ⅓ cup of glaze.

MEAT, POULTRY, OR GAME ASPIC

FOR 1 QUART:

2 leeks
1 tablespoon peanut oil
1 veal knuckle, chopped into pieces (see **Variations**)
2 calf's feet, chopped into pieces
2 carrots
1 bouquet garni
2 quarts water
1 onion
1 sprig tarragon
½ pound ground veal
1 egg white
Salt and pepper

COOKING:

Cut off and discard the greens from the leeks and wash the leeks. Heat the oil in a large pan over medium heat. Add the veal knuckle and calf's feet and brown them lightly. Add 1 of the leeks, 1 of the carrots, the bouquet garni, and the water. Bring to a boil, reduce the heat, and cook at a bare simmer, uncovered, for 12 hours, adding water occasionally to maintain the level of the liquid. Pour the stock through a fine sieve into a saucepan. Chill so that the fat comes to the surface and then remove the fat.

Chop the remaining leek and carrot, the onion, and the tarragon. Mix together the ground veal, the chopped vegetables and tarragon, and the egg white. You should get a loosely bound rather than compact mixture; if necessary add a bit of water. Stir this clarifying mixture into the strained stock. Set the pan over medium heat and bring it slowly to a boil. Lower the heat so that the stock just simmers and let it cook undisturbed for 20 minutes. Strain through a sieve lined with cheesecloth. Season the aspic with salt and pepper.

VARIATIONS:

For game aspic substitute venison trimmings for the veal knuckle.

For poultry aspic, replace the veal knuckle with a chicken, but do not brown it.

GAME STOCK

FOR 2 CUPS:

1¾ pounds carcasses or bones from game birds or animals
1 tablespoon oil
2 cups **mirepoix** (following recipe)
2 tablespoons cognac
2 cups wine
6 cups **veal stock** (page 234)

COOKING:

Heat the oven to 450°F. Put the oil and the carcasses or bones in a roasting pan and brown them in the oven for 30 minutes. Prepare the mirepoix. Pour the cognac over the warm mirepoix and flame. Scrape the bottom of the pan with a wooden spoon or spatula to dislodge any cooked-on juices. Remove the bones from the oven and pour the wine into the pan. Use either red or white wine depending on the dish to be made with the stock. Scrape the bottom of the roasting pan to dislodge any drippings.

Put the mirepoix and the bones and wine in a large pot and add the veal stock. Bring to boil and then reduce the heat and simmer for 4 hours. Skim often and, if necessary, add water during cooking.

Strain the stock into a bowl and refrigerate so that the fat comes to the surface. Remove the fat. If necessary, reduce the stock over high heat until it barely thickens and there are about 2 cups left. To check whether or not the stock is sufficiently reduced, put a bit of it on a chilled plate; it should congeal immediately.

MIREPOIX

FOR 2 CUPS:

1 leek
3 carrots
1 onion
1 shallot
1 tablespoon butter
1 bouquet garni

PREPARATIONS:

Cut off and discard the green top from the leek and wash the leek. Chop it and the carrots, onion, and shallot. In a small saucepan, melt the butter over low heat. Add the chopped vegetables and bouquet garni and cook until the vegetables are just lightly browned, 3 to 4 minutes. Remove the bouquet garni.

PEPPER SAUCE

FOR ⅓ CUP TO SERVE 4:

½ carrot
1 slice onion
1 slice leek
1 slice shallot
4 garlic cloves
1 teaspoon peppercorns
3 tablespoons butter
1 small bouquet garni
2 tablespoons cognac
1 tablespoon vinegar
1 cup **game stock** (page 236)
Salt and pepper

COOKING:

Chop the carrot, onion, leek, shallot, and garlic clove. Crush the peppercorns. In a small saucepan, melt ½ teaspoon of the butter over low heat. Add the chopped vegetables, the crushed pepper, and the bouquet garni and cook until the mixture begins to brown, 3 to 4 minutes. Pour the cognac over the vegetables and flame it. Continue cooking until all the liquid evaporates. Remove from the heat and add the vinegar and the game stock and then cook over low heat, uncovered, for 1 hour. Strain. You should have about ⅓ cup of sauce.

FINISHING:

Season the sauce with salt and pepper and add it to the pan used to cook the game or other meat with which you are serving the sauce. Bring to a boil, scraping the bottom of the pan to dislodge the drippings clinging to it. Thicken the sauce by whisking in the remaining butter and check the seasoning. The flavor of pepper should be pronounced.

Fonds d'artichauts

ARTICHOKE BOTTOMS

1 large onion
1 lemon
4 artichokes
½ to ¾ cup white wine
Salt and pepper

PREPARATIONS:

Slice the onion. Cut the lemon into halves. Prepare the artichokes by cutting the stems down to about ½ inch. Cut off the top two thirds of the artichoke leaves, or down to the fleshy bottom section of the artichokes. Remove the leaves from the artichoke bottoms by cutting down to the flesh with a sharp knife; hold the blade against the artichoke so that it points in the same direction as the leaves and cut through the leaves, turning the artichoke as if peeling an orange. Rub the cut lemon over each artichoke bottom as it is prepared, squeezing the lemon lightly to release some of the juice.

COOKING:

Spread the onion slices on the bottom of a saucepan and put the artichoke bottoms on top of them. Pour ½ inch of wine into the saucepan and then add water as needed to reach halfway up the artichokes. Season the artichokes with salt and pepper and simmer, covered, for 30 minutes. Let cool, remove the chokes, and return the artichoke bottoms to their liquid for storage.

RAVIOLI DOUGH

FOR ABOUT 1 POUND:

2 cups flour
3 eggs
1 pinch salt
Nutmeg

PREPARATIONS:

Put the flour, 1 of the eggs, and salt into a bowl. Grate a little nutmeg into the bowl and mix the ingredients slowly with a fork. When the first egg is absorbed, add the second, and then add the third. Knead the dough slowly at first and then more quickly until it forms a firm, elastic ball. Sprinkle with a little flour while kneading if the dough is sticky. Cover the dough with plastic wrap and let it rest 30 minutes in the refrigerator.

COMMENT: This pasta does not keep very long before drying out. To roll the dough, see page 81.

Pâte feuilletée

PUFF PASTRY

FOR ABOUT 2½ POUNDS:

1 cup cake flour (see **NOTE**)
3 cups all-purpose flour
¾ cup very cold water
1¼ pounds (5 sticks) butter
2 teaspoons salt

PREPARATIONS:

Put both flours, ¼ pound of the butter, and the salt in the food processor and whir a few seconds to distribute the butter. Add the cold water and process several seconds until thoroughly mixed. If the dough is very crumbly, add a tablespoon of water and whir briefly. In all, the dough should be processed only about ½ minute. Press it together into a ball, wrap it in a moist dish towel, and let it rest in the refrigerator for at least 3 hours.

Remove the dough from the refrigerator and let soften somewhat so that it is easy to roll. On a floured work surface, roll out the dough to form a rectangle approximately 12 inches by 22 inches. Cut the remaining pound of butter into slices about ⅛ inch thick and cover the dough with the butter, being careful to leave a ½-inch border.

Fold the border of dough over onto the butter. Position the dough so that the long edge of the rectangle faces you. Divide the pastry mentally into thirds and then fold the left third over onto the central third. Now fold the right-hand third over on top of the other two, making sure to align the sections carefully. You should have a rectangle with the short side facing you. You will use the flap, which is at your left, as a guide in the turning process.

Set the pastry so that the flap edge is in front of you and roll the pastry away from you to form a sheet about 12 inches long. Now is the beginning of the first double turn, which you will repeat three more times. Turn the pastry so that the flap edge (rolled out but visible) is on your left and roll out the pastry, away from you again, until it measures 30 inches in length. Use a ruler to push the edges of the pastry so that they are straight, and then turn the flap edge so that it is in front of you again. Now mentally divide the long side, which is facing you, in half. Fold over the left side so that the edge reaches the imaginary middle line of the pastry and then do the same with the right side. Now fold the right half over onto the left side, thus forming a new flap on the left. Make a finger mark in the pastry to signify that it has had one double turn, cover with plastic wrap, and set in the refrigerator to rest for at least 45 minutes.

Remove the dough from the refrigerator and give it a second double turn. Once more set the flap on your left. Roll the dough out to 30 inches and turn, so that the flap edge is in front of you. Fold both edges into the middle and then the right side over the left exactly as above. Mark with 2 fingers, wrap, and let it rest at least 45 minutes in the refrigerator.

Roll it and fold it again, as above, and mark the third double turn. Let it rest again before making the fourth and final double turn, following the same procedures as for the first three turns. When the puff pastry is finished, refrigerate, well wrapped, until just before using.

NOTE: *Cake flour does not appear in Fredy Girardet's recipe. It is used here because it yields the best result in combination with American all-purpose flour. Ed.*

Pâte sucrée

SWEET PASTRY

FOR 2 POUNDS:

10 ounces (2½ sticks) butter
4 cups flour
¾ cup sugar
1 pinch salt
1 whole egg
1 egg yolk

PREPARATIONS:

Put the butter, cut in pieces, the flour, the sugar, and the salt in a bowl and work together with your fingertips until the mixture is the consistency of meal. Mix in the whole egg and the yolk just until amalgamated. This is a dough that ought not to be overworked. Squeeze the dough together firmly so that it holds together in a ball. Cover with plastic wrap and let it rest a few hours in the refrigerator before using.

Génoise

SPONGE CAKE

TO SERVE 6:

3 eggs
⅔ cup sugar
1 cup flour
1 pinch salt

COOKING:

Heat the oven to 350°F. Cut an 8-inch round of sulfurized or waxed paper and put it on the bottom of a cake pan 8 inches in diameter and at least 2½ inches high. Break the eggs into a medium-size metal bowl, add the sugar, and put the bowl in a large pan of warm water over very low heat. Beat until frothy and lukewarm, 2 to 3 minutes. Remove the bowl from the water bath and continue to beat the mixture until it thickens and leaves a ribbon trail when the beaters are lifted, about 10 minutes in all. Mix the flour and salt together and fold them into the beaten eggs a third at a time.

Fill the prepared pan with the batter and bake the cake in the preheated oven for about 35 minutes. Give the pan a quarter turn two or three times during the cooking so that the cake cooks evenly. Run a knife around the edge of the pan and turn the cake out on a rack. Peel off the paper and let the cake cool.

CHOCOLATE SPONGE CAKE

TO SERVE 6:

¼ cup flour
¼ teaspoon salt
1 tablespoon unsweetened cocoa
⅓ cup ground almonds
3 eggs
6 tablespoons sugar

COOKING:

Heat the oven to 350°F. Cut an 8-inch round of sulfurized or waxed paper and put it on the bottom of a cake pan 8 inches in diameter and at least 2½ inches high. Mix the flour, salt, cocoa, and ground almonds in a bowl.

Put the eggs and sugar in a bowl and set this in a large pan of water. Heat so that the water bath is just simmering and start to beat the eggs and sugar. Continue beating until the mixture is lukewarm, 2 to 3 minutes. When it reaches this temperature, it will start to foam. Remove the bowl from the water bath and continue to beat the mixture until it thickens and leaves a ribbon trail when the beaters are lifted, about 10 minutes in all. With a spatula, fold the flour, salt, cocoa, and almonds into the egg mixture in three batches.

Fill the prepared cake pan with the batter and bake it in the preheated oven for about 35 minutes. Turn the pan two or three times as the cake bakes so that it cooks evenly. Run a knife around the edge of the pan and turn the cake out on a rack. Peel off the paper and leave the cake to cool.

Crème pâtissière

PASTRY CREAM

FOR APPROXIMATELY 2½ CUPS:

2 whole eggs
3 egg yolks
¾ cup sugar
1⅔ cups milk
½ vanilla bean
⅓ cup flour

COOKING:

Whisk together the whole eggs, egg yolks, and sugar until the mixture lightens in color and increases in volume. The eggs will expand more quickly if the bowl is set in a water bath over low heat while beating. Put the milk in a pan with the vanilla and bring to a boil. Pour the boiling milk over the beaten eggs and whisk together. Then add the flour. Put the mixture in a saucepan and bring it just to a boil over low heat, stirring. Remove it from the heat and strain it into a bowl through a fine sieve.

PRALINE

2 cups sugar
6 ounces (about 1¼ cups) whole almonds with skins
6 ounces (about 1¼ cups) whole hazelnuts with skins

PREPARATIONS:

Lightly oil a baking sheet. In a saucepan, melt the sugar over very low heat. Do not stir until the sugar starts to melt. As soon as the sugar has liquefied and turned caramel colored, quickly add to it as many of the almonds and hazelnuts as it will absorb. Pour the praline out onto the oiled baking sheet and set aside to harden.

FINISHING:

Break off one or more pieces and chop with a knife before adding to the recipe you are preparing. Store praline in an airtight container to protect it from humidity.

Glace royale

ROYAL ICING

1 ¼ cups powdered sugar
½ egg white
¼ lemon

PREPARATIONS:

In a bowl, mix the sugar and egg white together and then squeeze in ½ teaspoon lemon juice. If the icing is too liquid, add more sugar. Use immediately, or the icing can be kept for a short time if the bowl is covered with a damp cloth.

INDEX